praise for *you're* ᴗ

"Trying your best and just want someone to notice?
This book was written for you."
—anna przy,
author of *Keep It Up, Cutie: A Not Quite Self-Help Book*

"If you need an exhale and a laugh at the same time,
read this book."
—jess ekstrom,
author of *Chasing the Bright Side*

"Relatable, real, and a heart song for those of us
who dream big, love hard, and want to be our best while
fighting against all the voices that tell us who we are supposed
to be. Devrie makes you cry, laugh, and critically think
about who you were and who you want to be.
Do yourself a favor—read this!"
—barrett pall,
journalist, LGBTQIA+ advocate, life coach

"An incredible comfort and a stunning debut,
You're Gonna Die Alone is hope for the hopeless romantics
and the cheese-loving darlings…Hilarious, heartbreaking,
and hopeful. Just like life should be."
—alicia ross,
BookToker

"This book made me heartily laugh out loud! Devrie's humor is woven so stunningly and naturally throughout every chapter, even in the most devastating and crushing moments. It is full of sage advice and hard truths, but never pretentious or all-knowing."
—mary elizabeth kelly,
actor, writer, comedian

"I found myself laughing out loud, then crying tears I didn't know I had in me, then crying from hysterically laughing again, all while feeling fully seen. This is the book I needed to navigate growing up, the book I didn't know I needed at thirty years old, and the book I would gift to every woman in my life."
—brianna mcdonnell,
writer, actor, producer

"A collection of delicate and complex emotions shown under the softest of lights, handled with care, all while allowing you room to laugh and smile."
—naina singh,
songwriter, TikToker

"I've never read a book like this before. It flowed like a deep conversation with Devrie…She just GETS IT."
—jessy parr,
visual storyteller, IG influencer

"Devrie reaches across time and space to grab the hand of the scared and ashamed thirteen-year-old that lives within each of us...Equal parts time capsule, love letter, and permission slip, Devrie's story is delightfully funny and profoundly liberating."
—eliza day,
actor, writer, intuitive reader

"In a market flooded with self-help books, Devrie Donalson's excellently titled *You're Gonna Die Alone (& Other Excellent News)* stands out...From Tinder and tattoos to rejection and healing, Donalson's remarkable journey of discovery reveals a woman who has broken free of the baggage that had been weighing her down for so long."
—new york post

"[A] compassionate debut...Donalson's collection is a fierce declaration of self, it is also a map of the metamorphoses required for that self to exist. Readers seeking a relatable confession of self-discovery will find ample wisdom and laughs."
—publishers weekly

you're gonna die alone

(& other excellent news)

devrie brynn donalson

you're gonna die alone

(& other excellent news)

BLACK STONE
PUBLISHING

Printed in the United States of America
Originally published in hardcover by Blackstone Publishing in 2023

First paperback edition: 2024
ISBN 979-8-212-87711-4
Humor / Form / Essays

Version 1

Blackstone Publishing
31 Mistletoe Rd.
Ashland, OR 97520

www.BlackstonePublishing.com

To those with dirt beneath their nails:
You're my favorite type of people.
We're gonna be okay.

CONTENTS

read this first
(seriously)

You are welcome to never read this book. You might think it is a trite, unimportant, vacant collection of barely-thoughts from a sad, narcissistic internet clown. You might very possibly be right.

But there's a chance you might find it helpful, too.

If you're anything like me, you might struggle with knowing exactly what you want to do with your life, or exactly how to become who you want to be. You might find yourself wrestling with the push and pull of *knowing* you're a good person, but *feeling* like you're not. Maybe there are people in your life who you desperately want to approve of you, and who you love very much, but who remind you that there is always something here or there you should change. If you're anything like me, maybe that little voice reminding you that you aren't quite yet worthy of some kind of love or acceptance has kept you from saying yes to opportunities you wonder if you'll ever get again.

When I was finally forced to go from living a life half awake to actually being free, the things I discovered that were holding me back surprised me. I was a fiercely independent person, but I was desperately afraid of being abandoned. I was trying to be someone I could be proud of, but I was ashamed of who I had been. I was more afraid of failing than I was of never trying, and I would do anything to keep the people whose love I craved the most from realizing just how disappointing I'd become.

It wasn't easy and it wasn't clean, but I found my way out of a story I'd been told my entire life about who I was and what I needed to change to deserve a life that felt honest. From deconstructing the most basic understandings about men, women, and society to reconsidering the treatment so many of us endured as children, from raging against loss to accepting the grief of change, and from realizing I didn't recognize who I was anymore to rediscovering the most basic, fundamental truths of being human, I've been through a hell of a decade. I hope that sharing those stories now might find the one person out there who needs to hear them.

This book is simply an invitation for you to come and see what you find. You might find a few laughs, and you might realize that taking a break to laugh is exactly what you needed. You might find grief pressed between these pages and realize that you still have people, places, and memories to put to rest. You might find a bit of forgiveness and realize that you have been withholding it from yourself for far too long. You might find the courage to change.

What I *hope* you find if you decide to read on is this: a little grace, a little humor, and a whole lot of room to take a deep breath again. I hope you find peace. I hope you see that you can bet on yourself, even when the people you love the most haven't figured out how to bet on you yet. I hope you find the comfort of your own company, and when you do, I hope you find it to be *enough*.

You'll know what you need when you see it. Take what helps. Leave the rest.

P.S. Every editor who has read this book has made some version of the following comment:

"I thought I hated poetry, but now I have to reconsider my life choices. Damn you."

So. Read the poems, k? You'll probably like them.

P.P.S. Don't skip the footnotes—they're the heart and soul of this whole ridiculous mess.

a quick but important note

I only have my experience and perspective to share from. Let me acknowledge right off the bat that I know what I have personally experienced is not something that everyone has access to.

I won't talk too much about the intersections of privilege that have allowed my life to look the way it has so far. There are far more educated and talented people facilitating conversations around topics of identity and privilege, as well as the structural elements our society upholds to bar certain communities from having access to travel, economic stability, and safety.

I speak about the impact of the patriarchy and the relationships between men, women, and society. I try to acknowledge that I'm only speaking about a certain type of man, or qualify that I'm not including trans men in larger conversations about the monolith of cis-men behavior. I do not speak to the experience of people who aren't cis men and cis women, because they are not mine to speak to, but I want to acknowledge here that trans women are women, trans men are men, and all other gender identities are equally valid. I support trans people and their rights without exception. You are always welcome here.

I do not pretend to have all the answers, and I suspect by the time you're reading this there will be things in this book I might wish to have said differently, or not to have said at all. We are always changing, always learning, always growing. At least, I hope we are.

Lastly, the stories in this book are true to the best of my recollection, but who knows what goes on in the dark, swirly place where memories live? I'm doing my best. Names and details are changed, of course. You little snoop.

I think it's time . . .

I wish my fear of failure
was smaller than my fear
of a Too Small Life.

I admire so greatly
the people who *try* without any guarantee of success . . .

I wasn't born with that bone.

I've made myself small,
I've corralled myself in
trying to control the way that people see me,
and the bottom line is this:

I never will.

People will see me the way that they need to in order to carry on.

So,
I think it's time I stop seeing myself,
when I look in the mirror,
as a single pin on a paper map

but rather,

a galaxy with ever-unfurling edges.
Nothing staring back at me but the potential for vastness.
For the unexplored.
For the unending . . .

I think it's time to be brave.

furbys, beanie babies & other nasty lies

When I was a little girl in the 1990s, the Furby was *the* toy to have, for a brief, but very intense time. Furbys were animatronic creatures that were a cross between a gumdrop, a gremlin, and an owl, about the size of a toddler's head, with bright-red tongues tucked inside yellow clacking beaks. They would blink with an ominous *click* and yowl "Feed me!" in increasing volume until you physically pressed the tongue down to satiate their hunger. A Furby was more than a toy; it became a marker of social status in the nefarious way that expensive and ridiculous things become. In certain suburban households, a Christmas tree without a Furby underneath it was the fastest way to guarantee a matching-pajama-hot-cocoa-festive-morning meltdown. I became convinced that securing a Furby was the only way to secure the adoration and approval of my peers, and thus, I insisted on a trip to Toys "R" Us, lest my social status be defined by my pitiful, Furby-less existence. When I unwrapped that glistening box, squealing with troll-like glee, I had no idea what was coming for me.

Every child who fell prey to the clacking craze was destined to experience the same horrible, haunting event. The night when each Furby on the planet would come alive during the witching hour and wail, hungry and menacing, from the depths of whatever dark hole it was festering in:

"Feeeed me."

Every one of us would have to survive the Night of Endless Hunger.

My Furby, a powder-blue Baby Furby,[1] betrayed me from deep within my closet. Its keening tore me from my sleep during the wee hours, which is never really a good time to be awoken by a confusing closet demon. Petrified, with covers pulled up to my eyes, I listened to its bone-chilling beckoning, wincing with each increase in volume and bloodlust, and thinking that I was about to die.

Moments before I breathed what I was sure would be my last, my father burst into my room. He wore nothing but his standard sleep uniform of tighty-whities,[2] and he burned with the hatred of a man summoned by a yowling nightmare that already cost him way too many dollars, much less his sleep. We didn't speak a word to each other as he stood, frozen in place and listening. When the next La Llorona impression rose from the dark, his head whipped around, homing in on the most unwelcome mouth to feed. He flung open the closet door and disappeared into the black, matching the Furby's Antichrist energy and rummaging through the closet like a man possessed. The wailing became clearer and sharper as he hauled it from the depths of the stuffed animal pile in which it dwelled and held it up against the silver-gray light of the moon. Its feverish

---

1. Objectively better than other Furbys because it was smaller and cuter.
2. A state in which I'm sure he would have rather not been stampeding around in front of his child, but war makes tighty-whities-wearers of us all.

eyes locked on mine and blinked once as it built up another cry. Then my dad produced a screwdriver from a place I have never, ever wanted to know about, unscrewed the battery compartment, and ripped out its double-Ds.

The room fell silent. There was no sound but the heaving of my father's chest as he stared in the dark at the beast cradled in his hand, daring it to move.

The Furby was still. It was over.

He dropped his vanquished foe in disgust and left without a word, eking the door closed behind him and plunging me back into darkness to, presumably, get some sleep, but I was a child who had just witnessed an unholy war. There was no chance I was about to get sloppy by going night-night. Plus, I knew from a *lot* of Sunday school: the Devil don't go down easy. So I remained vigilant, encased in my terror, blankets up to my chin and ears alert. The air was still wrong. *Something was coming.*

I held my breath. Waited.

From the dark maw of my closet, it came. A distinct, crisp . . . *Clack.* Then in a long, low, distorted rumble:

"Feeeeeeeeeed Meeeeee."

Dear Reader, I may have shat the bed.

There wasn't much to do in the face of an undead-demonic owl toy but play dead and ponder the afterlife, so I was wondering how my family would write an obituary about a tragically young death brought on by a Furby when my door burst open again. Perhaps my dad had been hovering, waiting for the invading hellspawn to test him, or maybe he had ears like one of those blind fruit bats—either way, I was grateful. In one swift motion, my six-foot-three father—all long limbs, tight underpants, and coiled rage—reached down, snatched Lucifer's Canary off the ground, and hurled it at the wall. It collided with an audible *crack.*

There was the briefest moment of silence. The ragged breath of a man whose sanity was flirting unabashedly with the Void. Then, a bolt of fear as a different voice, laced with just as much danger, pierced through the night. *"Mark!"*

It was my mom. Another casualty of the age-old tale of man versus beast. The Furby might have been my dad's Moby Dick—his tiny, fuzzy, blue whale—but she was the mother of his children and the woman in his bed whom he'd just awoken *again* in his bananas vendetta against a child's toy. His head fell as he skulked away to try to explain what the very valid commotion was, closing the door behind him.

It should be noted that had he done this even days before the Night of Endless Hunger, there would have been hell to pay. He once stole my Christina Aguilera doll—complete with a pressable belly button that played a clip from "Genie in a Bottle" over and over through garbled speakers hidden in her boobs—and stashed her in the oven. I suppose he wanted a moment of relief from the same crackly verse jackhammering his eardrums for the thousandth time, but I could never forgive him. What if the oven had turned on? What if he had cremated X-Tina?! For just the possibility, he was a monster, and I didn't speak to him for a whole day, which is, like, a year in kid days. But for slaughtering my Baby Furby in front of my eyes? He was a goddamn hero. That's how truly harrowing this fucking thing was.

So there I was alone, peering through the dark, trying to discern a broken shape in the far corner of my room. I could just make out the pale-blue body in the slanting moonlight—a yellow beak slightly slack, a cherry tongue finally stilled, and a pair of wide, unblinking eyes.[3] The carnage stared back at me as

3. To the best of my knowledge, this memory—soaked in the adrenaline of fearing death, the religious trauma of the '90s Zealot Revival, and the imagination of a child who also believed (a probably racist) Br'er Fox lived in

I reckoned with my disappointment. Having a Baby Furby was supposed to be a key to having a good life, being liked and accepted, and being *safe* in the vicious halls of elementary school. It wasn't just a toy, it was a guarantee, promising to deliver both comfort *and* the envy of all my friends. But as the Night of Endless Hunger crystallized into a core childhood trauma, I realized that following the Furby rules of coolness hadn't brought me anything but the promise of future therapy.

I should have known then and there: don't trust the hype, especially around '90s toys.

But setting healthy boundaries has never been my strong suit.

Enter: Beanie Babies. They were different than the Furbys in almost every way. They were cute and simple, without a single battery or speaker. They were tried and true and they never haunted children. They had different personalities and vibes, and the Beanie Baby you brought to school in your backpack said a ton about who you were as a person. They were approachable, collectible, and constantly surprising you with new releases to keep your interest. Furbys were out, and Beanies were in. If you wanted to be a somebody who was anybody at all, you needed *at least* one enviable Beanie Baby. In short, they were *the shit*.

By the height of their fame, I had amassed a collection that could fill an entire storage bin. I was a spoiled child of upper-middle-class white suburbia, so the lesson of the Furby was long forgotten. Beanie Babies promised to secure my place as an "It Girl," and that meant security all the way around. Like

---

her attic and would kill her any night now—is one hundred percent true. My father, on the other hand, remembers it slightly differently, but he is infamous for having the worst memory in the family. So you be the judge.

everyone else who's ever been a kid who wanted to fit in, I was going to take any chance I could to ensure my place in the hierarchy developing around me.

And the best part? Beanies were *fun*. My best friend and I spent years of our lives "playing Beanie Babies." We'd sprawl out on the floor in front of a massive pile of little plush bodies and take turns picking which Beanies each one of us got to voice that day, like we were team captains choosing out of a lineup for kickball. We whittled away the ticking clock of childhood constructing plots and subplots and sub-subplots to rival the steamiest soap, laced with politics, backstabbing, drama, heartbreak, and love. Our stories could have made the *Game of Thrones* writers blush and say, "Is that a bit much, do you think?" No, you coward, *I don't think*. The world of Beanie Babies was a cutthroat place, full of lust and blood and high school mean girls, and we were their gods.

Our time as residents of Beanie Olympus came to an abrupt halt the day *someone* decided that Beanie Babies were the newest investment craze. In the frenzy of the Princess Diana Bear, which came out in memoriam of the British royal who had died too young and too tragically, it became common knowledge that if you kept your Beanies in pristine condition, you would be able to sell them someday to a grown adult with a lot of money and a deep love of children's toys. In fact, rumor was you'd be able to sell them for more cashola than you'd seen in your entire life. Everyone said so, and as the Beanie Investment Craze spread, more and more people started boxing up their Beanies and selling out stores. Suddenly Mystic the Unicorn and Peanut the Elephant weren't just head cheerleaders of Beanie High cheating on their boyfriends with their boyfriends' brothers, they were our future college tuition. Fuzzy little bags of janglin' coin. A practical guarantee.

And so, overnight, we didn't play Beanie Babies anymore.

While I hadn't yet achieved popular-girl status through my ever-growing stash, this new promise of an even greater security was too tempting to resist. The Beanies were put into the storage bin, lifted high above my head on the top shelf of the closet, and left to appreciate in value even if their tags were a little bent and their fur was a little matted. We moved on to bigger and better things like making potions in the backyard out of plants and water and dirt. We played kickball against the garage and poured hours into choreographing dance routines. Sometimes I would gaze longingly up at the bin, pining for days spent at Beanie High while our imaginations ran wild and free, but my future was more important than fleeting flights of sentimental fancy. I had to sacrifice if I wanted to be successful.

The Beanies rested above me, watching me go through phase after phase: getting braces on, falling in love to fall out of it just as fast, getting braces off, making out with my mirror and watching the kiss in *Cinderella Story* over and over because you can see a tiny bit of Chad Michael Murray's tongue if you watch *really* closely.[4] They saw me study for tests, and slam my door, and giggle all night during sleepovers. They watched me put on my graduation robes and pack moving boxes for the first time. Then, they didn't watch me at all anymore unless I came home from college on weekends. By the time I moved away, I'd forgotten about them completely, but that was okay, they'd already seen me grow up.

Well, Dear Reader, I'm sure I don't have to tell you that life comes at you fast and hard once you leave the mythical lands of childhood.[5] Get a few years on you, and your tags get bent. Your

---

4. You're gonna go look, aren't you? You little perv—I love it.
5. Everything gets a little bit harder when you become an adult and lose the magical thinking of being a child, even if you experienced stability in many areas of your life.

fur gets a little matted. So I found myself, midtwenties making shit money at a part-time job I'd been doing at least a year too long, in desperate need of some magic. One day I sat in the boiling seat of my un-air-conditioned car on my fourth Del Taco dollar-menu lunch of the week, watching the clock tick away the minutes of my pitiful break, and wondered how the hell I was gonna get out of there and turn my life into something I was happy living. I didn't have a plan, I didn't have money, and I didn't have the heart to go back to the world of corporate bullshit that had already taken years off my life. I needed a swift inheritance—or a goose that laid hair color so I could stop spending money to keep my dishwater-blond roots at bay—and I needed it fast. As I sat idly counting the appalling amount of lifted trucks with *Don't Tread On Me* flags littering the parking lot, a thought came to me as though from the heavens. No, not *the* heavens— *my* heavens. Beanie Olympus, where I was once a god.

Holy shit, the Beanies.

The moneybags of my forgotten youth were still suspended in time, Pompeii-style, in my childhood room. Those fancy little fluffs! I briefly wondered why no one was talking about their Beanie Babies windfalls, or the way they'd named their first yacht *Pincher* after the über-rare lobster baby that had single-clawdedly funded the vessel with the price it had fetched on eBay, but I quickly dismissed the concern. In my desperation, I figured I was probably just smarter than everyone who had forgotten about their squirreled-away fortune. I was just special, and this was gonna work.

I dropped the burrito and whipped open a new search window to type greedily, *How much are Beanie Babies worth?* I felt vindicated and deserving. After all, I had been patient. I had sacrificed. I'd followed the rules, and it was about to pay off.

Have you ever been really, really hungry, and specifically

craving, like, *that one* sandwich you had a million years ago that was the best sandwich you've ever tasted, so you hunt it down and you order it? And when it comes you're like *oh my god this is it. This is going to satiate the hunger that has been wearing away my insides since I had this as a child. I am finally about to feel whole. My life is going to be perfect. I'm going to fire my therapist.* Then you take a bite and it's the worst sandwich you've ever had? Like how Subway always *smells* amazing, then it enters your body and you can feel the years of your life being stripped away by their mystery-fish-mash?[6]

The moment I Googled the price of Beanie Babies on the internet as a full-grown adult was a lot like the first bite of a devastatingly disappointing sandwich. At the time of this writing, the Princess Diana Beanie Baby—the cream of the crop and guaranteed windfall—is going for between five dollars and one hundred dollars on the internet.

As I stared at my phone, a wave of grief and anger washed over me. I know this sounds like a disproportionate response to learning the Beanie Babies I was completely unaware of until moments before were not going to fetch me Taylor Swift's Rhode Island house–money, but I implore you to remember I was eating my fourth helping for the week of cheap beans in a sweltering car, and Diana Bear was doing me dirty. This was supposed to be my inheritance! My insurance! My retirement! My first yacht!

RIP to my yacht, *Pincher.* Ye never even saw the sea.[7]

I was flooded with indignance. What, exactly, had I given it all up for? All those days I gazed after my childhood with wanderlust, seeing the Beanies pressed together in the airtight

---

6. The fact that there is still much debate over exactly *what* Subway's "tuna" is fills me with giddy, nasty joy.

7. This is meant to be read in a pirate accent and if you didn't do that right off the bat . . . I'm not sure about you.

tub in which they'd been entombed, wishing I didn't have to let them go, and dancing horribly to Hilary Duff?

I had been promised security and safety. I had been promised a world that made sense, where I had everything I wanted, and where I didn't have to worry about affording the fast-food burrito with beef in it and not just beans. I had been promised my sacrifices were guaranteed to pay off in the end.

My Furby only brought me fear, not friends. My Beanie Babies didn't earn me Most Popular. They didn't even earn me the cost of a tank of gas.

It had all been a lie. The toys and trappings I'd been promised would deliver me a perfect life *didn't*. And when I thought about it, neither had my bachelor's degree or my master's degree. I had been heartily promised by every adult in the entire effing cosmos that higher education was the only route to being forever more secure than those without. But my part-time, sweaty butt was certainly *not* earning Manhattan high-rise money while classmates who skipped college were counting pennies. Two degrees hadn't launched me into the orbit of the successful and carefree. Neither had the years of fun and play I'd given up, or the things I'd surrounded myself with as a shield from insecurity. Neither had all the boys I hadn't kissed, or all the drinks I hadn't sneaked, or all the pounds I'd lost and gained and lost again. I was still there, with not enough money and a heart that had been mangled in a million ways, counting my sacrifices on my fingers with nothing to show for them.

I followed all the rules. I did what I was supposed to, and it didn't fucking matter, I thought to myself. *Rules might be . . . bullshit?*

Have you ever had a favorite sweater and been reeeaaaal stoked on it, like this is a GREAT sweater that looks GREAT on you and you wear it all the time, and then you find a Judas-ass rogue thread. So you pull the thread because *we don't abide rebel threads*, but the thread doesn't snap. The thread keeps coming. And you realize *oh shit, it's one of those threads*—but it's too late. It's been pulled. And before your very eyes the sweater that was your favorite thing to cover up in to feel comfy and safe unravels around you?

This was kind of like that, but the sweater is life, man. Life and all the things I thought were true because of my blind trust in the *rules*. As I held the remains of what I thought to be true in my hands, I realized that the realization had loosened a hard-to-see thread.

Learning that the promised trade-off for rule-following was not *actually* promised at all revealed the constant current—slow, deep, and strong—that ran beneath everything I had done in my life. It was the beliefs that influenced every decision I made. It might not have been as flashy as the riptide or the white water, but it had moved me unnoticed, and I'd been none the wiser. Sometimes when I was little I'd be playing in the ocean, splashing and swimming and watching the sunlight catch on the droplets, and then I'd look back and realize I'd drifted a really long way from my beach chair on the shore. Sometimes life is like that. We don't realize that something is tugging us toward a place we never meant to go until, one day, we're just . . . there. Drawn by a quiet current made of our sacrifices and belief in other people's stories about what to do with our lives.

The truth is, very few of the ways we are convinced to sacrifice our wonderful and colorful desires in exchange for something secure *actually* end up leaving us with anything that looks like security. I can't think of even one of those promises that really came through except maybe, like, not trying heroin. Not trying heroin still feels like solid advice. But really, most of the things we were taught about going to college and not messing around under the bleachers and not moving too far away and not skipping church and not touching our Beanie Babies since they're gonna make us rich only serve to make our world a little smaller. It's a bad trade. All this giving up—and for what purpose? Who benefits from our outline being drawn harder and darker into the pages of the Book of the Way Things Are when our sacrifices only make us smaller?

Nothing can guarantee us a "perfect future" if a "perfect future" means security. We can only control what we can. We can only decide what we are willing to sacrifice.

The Furby, the Beanie Babies, and all the other things that had promised one thing and delivered another piled up in front of me. I saw the current pulling me toward a life of wanting safety over freedom, and I decided to make one more sacrifice. I would sacrifice the feeling safe if it meant finally feeling real.

I'm sure I will relapse into my security-craving ways many times in my life, but I *hope* I keep adding gray hair to the head of my financial advisor[8] and doing whatever makes me feel like this life is worth all the heart-wrenching bits. I'll choose a future full of color and hope and love and living, because the loss and fear and dying is guaranteed, and none of us make it out without a bent tag here or some matted fur there. If we want a kaleidoscope story instead of the black and gray resentment for the things we gave up and never got back, we have to reject the greater stories that argue Safety over Everything. We have to reject the story that following the rules is the only way to get out unscathed.

Let this Furby survivor tell you: don't believe the hype. Not all rules are made the same, and some are meant to be broken.

---

8. Bahahaha I don't have a financial advisor.

Edinburgh

It is
The hours when no one else is awake
The mist rising from the cobblestones
The last of the tears as the daylight breaks
A mantra, a plea, and prayer: home?

The halfway there of burning lungs
The steady quiet of a place so old
The wall where all my regrets are hung
A thawing heart in the winter cold

The blooming yellow of a changing tide
The persistent call of a soaring gull
The budding pink hope of a stubborn pride
A living room, plate, and glass half full

The sudden relief of the breakthrough sun
The music of artists come to play
The warmest place a black sheep could run
A starting over come to stay

It is
The hours when no one else is awake
The mist rising from the cobblestones
The joy in the tears as the daylight breaks
A knowing, a finding, a triumph: home.

scotland, grief & the vibrator in my grandma's garage

I never thought of myself as being afraid of being abandoned. In fact, I prided myself on being fiercely independent and capable of handling myself. I wasn't the sort to fall to pieces when things went wrong. I knew women like that, and I was nothing like them. I was the person people called on when shit hit the fan, and my inner circle was as close to me as blood. People with abandonment issues were people pleasers and pushovers, or reclusive, cold introverts, and neither type had the sort of bulletproof friendships I had kept for over twenty years. Sure, I didn't like being alone, but I was an extrovert who loved to have good company. That wasn't the same as the type of girls who accept any caliber of affection so they don't have to face themselves. I was nothing like them.

At least, that's what I thought before I was left behind.

———

"I have to go help Grandpa," my dad said, slipping on a flip-flop late at night. "Apparently he's sick to his stomach and weak.

I'm gonna go help him get downstairs and maybe take him to the ER." There was a tightness in his movement that betrayed his worry.

My dad's the sort of man who insists on not panicking until there's something to panic about, and even sometimes when there is. While I sat on the floor cross-legged, petting two happy, wagging dogs and ignoring one massive pit in my stomach, I had a bad feeling about the night—about the way my dad was moving. Maybe his body knew before he did that this wasn't a normal errand to help his aging father. Maybe mine did, too.

It was the height of Covid, so no one was allowed to go into the hospital with Grandpa, even though he was so unwell he was incapable of telling the doctors what was going on. He was sent home fairly quickly with antacids and some Tylenol. An hour later he was vomiting blood and couldn't speak with any sense.

We called another ambulance, but by the time he got back to the hospital and was given the proper examination, it was too late. The spontaneous brain bleed had been spilling into his skull for hours, eventually sending him into unconsciousness.

The next morning I went into work and wept into a flower arrangement. I tried, over and over, to place the last orange and black tiger lily into the nest of color, pulling my hand back only to watch the lily swing too low or turn too far to the side. Tiger lilies, despite their names, are delicate things. You can't handle them roughly the way you might a sturdier flower, like a rose. Lilies bruise if you look at them the wrong way.

"Come on," I cried over the thing, "Please, *please, just stay.*"

"Devrie." My boss put a hand on my shoulder. "Go."

"I just need to finish this," I sniffled back. "I have to finish this."

She reached forward and took the flower out of my hand. "You don't need to finish anything. You need to go."

At 10:00 a.m. we finally got a call from the doctor. I opened my messages and clicked on the family group text, blinking tears down my cheeks.

"This is it. We're saying goodbye to Grandpa."

———

We put on three masks each and waited in the lobby for our turn to go say goodbye to the patriarch of our family. We had to go in pairs of two, and when it was my brother's and my turn, I locked myself in the bathroom of Grandpa's hospital room and turned on the sink so my brother could grieve out loud and alone. Then we swapped, and I could hear his heart breaking in the sterile, gray restroom as I sat by my grandpa's bed and watched the man who'd been so tall and steady my entire life rattle shaky breaths in and out of his frail-looking body.

My grandpa was never one for too much affection. His hugs were always a little stiff, and he never was the one to initiate. The only time I remember him saying "I love you" was as he closed the door behind him the last time he was going to see me before I moved to another country for a year. He was the sort of man who loved you by always answering the phone, by being at every big game, and by putting air in your tires while you watched a movie inside. He was the sort of man who loved you by always being there to take care of you.

As I held his hand in mine at his deathbed, I offered a silent apology in my head for the awkward touch, and I spoke my gratitude from my heart out loud. I told him that I was proud to be his granddaughter and that I was proud to share his name. I thanked him for the ways he'd held the walls up when the wind was tearing through our house. I told him it was okay, that we'd take care of Nana, and that he'd been everything I needed him to be.

Then I leaned in really close and asked in a whisper just in case my brother could hear, "Please, *please, stay.*"

Later that day, I stopped by their house to leave the bananas he ate every morning on the counter, like he might come back and need his breakfast like normal. There was a photo there of my grandpa as a child, he couldn't have been more than five years old, wearing a cowboy hat, a kerchief, and a matching cow-print vest and fringe chaps over his jeans. His cat, long since buried in a backyard somewhere, was on the ground next to him looking very disgruntled with a toy lasso around its belly. My grandpa's face was split in a wide grin, his little fist wrapped around the rope that held his heifer against her will, looking like he'd won the first prize at the county fair. I took a photo of the picture with my phone.

The next morning I woke with a start and sat straight up, listening for whatever had pulled me from my fitful sleep, but there was no sound. I checked the clock to see that it was 7:15 a.m. I couldn't go back to dreaming. Instead, I looked at the image of Grandpa as a child on my phone, and I wondered what the cat was named.

When the doctor finally had the chance to call hours later, she told us that he'd passed away at 7:15 a.m. Nana would tell me in the months following that an orange and black butterfly had come into the garden around the same time and stayed for far longer than butterflies usually stay.

We spent the next few weeks packing up Grandpa's life. The night we went to the airplane hangar where he'd built a little museum and stored all his most important treasures, I was swept away with grief. I played "Brandy (You're a Fine Girl)" on his old jukebox as I spun through the space, tears pouring down my face and dust coating the tips of my fingers from trailing them along all the things he'd loved and saved.

We gathered his memory into our arms and brought it home to nestle away, to cherish, to lightly touch when no one else was looking. I tucked a black-and-white photo of him into an empty picture frame—a college student wearing a sleeveless tank and a knit hat with a little poof ball on top, focused and sure and steady, like he'd been his whole life. I surrounded that photo with a clock I knew he loved; an old, peeling leather record box from his house; and a framed photo of him grinning over his shoulder as he climbed into the cockpit of a fighter jet. It still didn't feel like enough. I couldn't believe he was gone.

I had never learned to grieve—much less to let go.

———

A year and a half later, I was in the exact same place—same job, same living situation, same everything. I'd felt the urgent call to find something more when my grandpa died so suddenly, but I hadn't acted on it. I didn't know what or how to change, and eventually the uncomfortable nagging in my heart that I was avoiding something important faded quietly enough into the background that I could ignore it. I was approaching my thirtieth birthday, stuck between clinging to someone I had always been and the persistent, whispering call of becoming someone new, when a new loss forced my hand.

My young life wasn't always stable or safe. My family and I experienced the fallout of mental illness and addiction in visceral, unrelenting ways. The only truly consistent people in my life were my grandparents and my closest childhood friends who had been with me from the time before we hit double digits. There were three of us, and we grew up together the best we could. I didn't have sisters, but I had them, and it felt the same to me. We were the sort of friends who came on each other's family vacations, whose houses we ended up at when something bad was happening in our own, and who were all referred to as the "extra daughter" by each other's parents. Even when other long friendships in my life had ended as we all grew up and grew apart, I never stopped counting on the two of them to be there, just like I was when they needed me. I'm a believer in platonic soulmates that come as friends, and the two of them were mine.

Then, one day, my two childhood best friends decided I shouldn't be in their lives anymore. One ending had been coming for a while, despite my most desperate attempts to save it, but the friendship had finally taken its last, devastating breath. The other ending blindsided me so abruptly it knocked me off my feet, and the two of them combined devastated me. Everything I knew before had been turned upside down in the wake of COVID-19. My two most vital friendships—those with the people whose houses had been the place of my first sleepovers and first PG-13 movies, who I had texted in a rush after my first kiss, whose hands I had held through their first heartbreaks, who sat next to me at our high school graduation, whose bridal showers I had hosted and wedding toasts I had written—were over. I didn't understand. I *couldn't*. The people I loved most in the world didn't want me anymore, and I couldn't change it. They thought I was someone I didn't think I was, but they didn't want me to explain why it wasn't true. They were just done—one with an explanation, and one without any at all. All my life I'd been a fighter, loyal to a fault and until the bitter end, but it hadn't been enough when the final moments came. They were leaving me behind.

During the fallout, I barely recognized myself when I looked in the mirror. I'd entered the period when the people you've always loved and counted on can't stay. Grandparents died. Friends left. When people you love stop loving you, there is nothing you can do. I didn't know how to let go, or if I should let go, or if I'd ever be able to walk the world alone. I only knew that it seemed like I might have to.

I didn't know who I was anymore. I *thought* I was a good person and a good friend, but so many people had cut me out of their lives without any real explanation, or with a confusing story about how it was somehow my fault. I asked my remaining friends point blank, "Am I awful? Am I a narcissist, or delusional, or abusive? What is wrong with me? Why won't anyone tell me? Why won't anyone stay?" They assured me that I was good, and I worked so hard to *be* good, and they didn't know why I had such a brutal track record. But if I *was* an awful, delusional, abusive narcissist, they wouldn't be able to tell me the truth, anyway, right?

I was overwhelmed with self-doubt. Who was I if the people who had known me the longest, who I had given all of my love and care over the course of my life, could find me so easy to leave behind? I was disoriented, feeling my way through the dark and hoping to find my way back to a world that made sense—where they would be waiting to say "Psych!" I waited for them to come back, but they didn't. I waited for them to come through, but they didn't. I couldn't have put my finger on it then, but the truth was my stability was gone. I was supposed to be the strong one, independent and capable, but in that moment my reflection was so, so scared. I was shaking and small, unable to move or breathe or think in a world where I had been abandoned.

So I decided I'd go somewhere new where no one knew my name, and face myself, because I thought I must have had something to learn. I didn't know if I would be able to land on my feet if I leaped without a plan, but the worst that could happen already had—I'd already lost the people that I thought would never leave me. I needed to find out who I *really* was, and I had to do it honestly. If I didn't, I would never stop feeling like I wasn't a gasping, toxic monster under all my loved ones' beds. I booked a flight to Scotland on a whim, running away from the growing collection of losses and fears and toward a timid hope.

The first time I stepped onto Scottish soil when I was seventeen, I'd experienced a rush—like a wind blowing up through my bones—that felt like some calling magic. I was only there a few days on a family vacation, but I swore I'd go back someday. In my early twenties, I backpacked through Europe, and I made sure to revisit the country that had spoken to me before. As I stood in front of Edinburgh Castle, I made a promise to the night that I'd be back and stay for longer. A few years later, I decided to get a master's degree, and I chose the University of Glasgow. I spent a year in Glasgow learning, and changing, and being incensed I'd never seen one of the foxes everyone told me roamed the city, before I had to come back home. The night before I left in 2017, I walked the streets alone while the softest, misty rain fell in a constant, quiet sheet. I listened to a love song called "Caledonia" while I sang along and cried, asking the universe for a sign. When a fox walked out of a dark alley and sat directly under the only streetlight ahead of me, I felt the rush blow through my bones again. We watched each other for a moment through the drops that looked like they were suspended in time, and I knew I wasn't done with that magical place yet.

It had been five years since I'd first chosen Scotland as a place to learn and let go. I had a few friends left in Glasgow, and a few in England, but I didn't know anyone in Edinburgh. I wanted to go somewhere I couldn't rely on the connections I'd made before, but hopefully had someone close enough to call in case of an emergency. I crossed my fingers that the friends I hadn't seen in so many years would take pity on me and planned a few days in Glasgow before I would go spend my birthday alone in Edinburgh. I'd only spent a day or two at a time there, scattered over more than ten years. Edinburgh was a city that didn't know me, and that I didn't know, but I hoped I might discover us both.

Scotland found me dizzy and stumbling, my self-trust completely destroyed in the wake of the messy, painful, confusing endings. With a heart splintered into a thousand pieces, I offered the bits of me up to the wind and the water like a sacrifice, praying it would be enough to stop the pain. I poured my sorrow out into my hands while I paced the cobblestone streets, letting it overflow and be carried away in the little rivers of Scottish rain that carve their way through the city and back to the sea. I left my grief tucked into the cracks of moss-covered stones, heather-covered earth, and worn pub booths. Swaying in the shadow of Edinburgh Castle, I held myself tightly and asked the birds what made me a person who is so easy to leave—just before they flew away. I toasted gin and tonics to the bitter freedom in being abandoned before tucking back into a damp apartment to cry alone. I let snowflakes melt in my hair while I took in the inky sky and thought about how they are so temporary. I stared into the winter sun that broke through the clouds over the crests of the highland mountains, begging the wild to numb me. I didn't tell many people why I was hurting, just that my life wasn't what I wanted it to be. The truth of my loss, my shame, only came out at night after a drink or two. My pain was a thing that howls at the moon.

Despite it, slowly, in fits and starts, I started to heal.

I bowled one of the worst games of my life in Glasgow surrounded by the people I'd known five years before when I first came to Scotland. People who had dropped everything to rally around their wayward, broken, lonely friend after so many years, and to fill her with pancakes and the warm glow of camaraderie.

As we walked through the botanic gardens together with frozen hands and toes, I told them about the flowers we were passing and about the people who were no longer blooming in my life, and wondered if maybe I was bad soil. They reminded me that some plants, no matter how hard you try, just want to fucking die. I should try not to take it personally.

A dear friend in London asked me to come celebrate my thirtieth birthday a few days late. I limped into her living room with a big smile, but I was barely being held together by chewed gum and Adele's *30* album on loop, and she knew it. Instead of asking, she took me out to dinner, and she plied me with perfectly chilled vodka, and then she leaned in the doorway with fogging breath while I laid on the frozen ground in my bra and underwear and wept as the neighborhood cat hopped over the fence back into his yard, because *he* was leaving me, too. In the morning when I asked her why my scarf had so many little twigs and shit tangled into it, she told me that I am not hard to love, but I am hard to walk home.

Two more friends I had scarcely seen or spoken to in years and who didn't know each other at all agreed to meet me in Bath. Us three women, all from such different worlds, battled our way through the sobering English rain, promenading around the Royal Crescent and doing our best *Bridgerton* impressions. We ended the day with wild hair and wild eyes, pulling period costumes over our soaking clothes and laughing maniacally as we curtseyed into a mirror at the Jane Austen museum. Later, after we all boarded our different trains, I cried again, but they were new tears—tears of wonder for the way that the love we deserve might only be able to find us once we make it room.

In between and after the bright spots spent with friends, I spent my time alone. Stubborn and determined, I made it back to Scotland after my heartsore couch surfing through England,

and on the wave of graciousness and kindness of so many strangers,[1] I found a place to live. I huffed my way up the hills of Edinburgh with massive IKEA bags, stuffed to the brim with light bulbs and blankets and toilet paper. I sat in restaurants and pubs by myself, tracing sad faces in the dripping condensation of my glass while I listened to tables of friends laugh over their after-work drinks. I booked tours on weekends and went on them alone, soaking up everything I could about the magical place that was nursing me back to life. I wandered the streets and learned to use the buses, and felt just like Cameron Diaz in *The Holiday* driving a rental car through little villages for a solo road trip. (I only scraped the car against something once.) I watched the birds out my back window tear up my flower beds and gave them names and scandalous backstories. I decided I'd write a book. Many of these pages were penned with only the company of a particularly fat pigeon and a particularly scrawny squirrel, who stole the pigeon's snacks every day.

I cautiously met—and trusted—new people, and they showed up for me in ways I'd never experienced before.[2] I found myself in Costco, sampling the much better food court[3] with friends from home who'd only been in my life a year or so, but who *wanted* to be there. The people I met in Scotland brought me out of my shell, drove me to secret spots, and told me drunken stories late into the night. Between finding new

1. After my birthday video went viral on TikTok, enough literal strangers sent me beer money that I went from broke to being able to rent an apartment for six months. I'll never get over that unearned generosity, or the way the universe saw me suffering and sent its best to lift me out of the water long enough for me to catch my breath. If you are one of the people who helped me, you are so beautiful. Thank you, thank you, thank you.

2. To the one who took care of me through a mail slot for the ten days I was alone and isolated with Covid—you're an actual hero.

3. Baked potatoes absolutely loaded with chili. Steak pies. Korean beef wraps.

friends, I started enjoying my time alone, wandering and learning and soaking in the world around me. For the first time, I relished my own company, and I relished my peace.

I maxed out the number of days I was allowed to stay without a permanent visa, and I boarded a plane to leave. I landed back in California an entirely different person than I'd been when I ran away six months before, and I let out a massive sigh of relief as I shrugged my unbelievably heavy carry-on off my back.

When I looked around my room, I noticed something I hadn't noticed before.

It was sort of a shrine to my grandpa.

My shelves were covered in his things and photos, taking up the places where things *I* loved used to be. Grandpa's treasures had collected a layer of dust just like the one they wore the night I'd collected them and held them to my chest as if I might keep him alive if I was gentle enough. After my grandpa died, it felt right, *necessary*, to keep those things and keep them close, so I sat with him watching over me for a year and a half before I left for Scotland. But after all that time learning to accept that nothing is guaranteed to stay and that I could be okay alone, I came home with new eyes and a new sense of balance. It was time to pack away some of Grandpa's things. It was time to make space for something new.

———

Two months later, I was doing well—except on nights I fell asleep anxious and had nightmares that my best friends were back in my life, even though they always left by the end. I woke up alone again and again, but I was okay with that. I had worked *so hard* to get okay with that. I woke up alone, and that was fine. I'd probably die alone, and that was fine, too.

Then my maternal grandma had a fall. She would recover, but she had lived alone since her husband, my other grandfather, died when I was thirteen. She decided it was time to sell the house and move into a retirement community. When I'd moved away for my master's degree, I'd stored boxes in her garage and hadn't touched them since. So I was back, ready to say goodbye to the house I'd spent every Christmas morning in and to finally go through the boxes of who-knew-what that I'd left collecting dust. The only thing I knew for a fact was in there was the first vibrator I'd ever bought, stashed away in a panic. I didn't know if you could fly with a vibrator, and I was not about to take the risk of a TSA agent at LAX waving around something pink and phallic and shouting "WHOSE BAG IS THIS?" So I hid it in my grandma's garage and prayed she would be able to control her nosy tendencies.

Beyond the cheap thrill and maybe a black widow or two, I wasn't expecting anything particularly devastating.

Then I opened the first box. It was like a time capsule grief bomb tore through me. Photo after photo of the friends who I'd lost just before I turned thirty—the ones that sent me running to Scotland to escape the pain—were stacked inside. Notes and drawings they'd made me were hidden between the glossy memories, all of them covered in dates going back to when we were only four years old. There were diaries we'd kept together, filling the pages with the boys we'd liked and the ratings we'd given them on critical things like "cuteness" and "athletic ability." Letters we'd written to each other when we'd moved apart mingled with birthday cards, gifts, and special trinkets I'd saved because they'd brought them home for me from family vacations.

As I reached into the boxes again and again, unearthing things I'd buried a long time ago, I felt like the hurt was brand new. Each photo came with a rush of smell, of sound, as I was swept up into the memories of a life we'd lived together. It was a record of my milestones—graduations and birthdays and big moments—and not one of the photos was of only me. Each one, for every important snapshot of my life, showed me with my arm around *them*.

I hovered over the two bins I'd set up—Trash or Keep—biting back the rushing tide that was lapping at my heart. I had worked so hard to heal from them, from their absence, from their need to be free of me. I was at peace, and I believed that for whatever reason they left, it must have been important. I didn't feel the need to understand anymore, and I didn't feel the need to explain to them why I said or did things I said or did, trying to guess at the moment they decided I wasn't worth the cost of knowing. I wanted them to be happy and free. If that meant a life without me, then I was happy for them.

But my hands were shaking because all that hard work disappeared in an instant. I had packed those boxes away when I had two best friends who had been my people my entire life, and who would be my people until we got old and died. The girl who'd shoved those boxes into her grandma's garage was a girl who knew that she'd be okay no matter what life threw at her, because those three friends had each other, and that was never going to change.

I opened those boxes as a person who didn't have childhood best friends anymore. A person who was learning that the only constant *was* change. In the time that we'd been apart, I'd realized that the ways they treated me weren't always very kind or very compassionate and that I had taken the fall for a lot of things they couldn't face about themselves. When there was friction, I was the only one left wondering if I was a good or a bad person, and I'd learned that *that* wasn't the sign of a very healthy friendship. I finally saw that the dynamics I'd seen as an indication of our bonds had really indicated my fear of being abandoned and my willingness to betray myself if it meant I would be *good enough*. I knew I never wanted that again, but even though I was healing, I was still sometimes hurting from the empty places they'd left behind.

As my hand moved toward the trash can to let all those memories go, I just couldn't do it. I wasn't ready to let *them* go. I wasn't ready to let *me* go—the me in those photos, who never imagined when she was packing those boxes that she was really packing a tomb. So I slid the papers and prints into the cracks of the Keep box that was filling up with the few things I wanted to save.

I haven't opened it since.

I haven't looked at the photos, or gone through the cards, or read the old diaries. I'm not sure if I ever will, or if someday I'll walk into the room with a new sense of balance and new eyes and wonder why I packed up a shrine to people who left my life so long ago. Maybe I'll open the box, pull out the photos, and be able to smile and be thankful for the people who put so much of me together while we grew up. Maybe their memories will leave me thankful for the lesson that taught me it's better to be abandoned than to abandon myself. Will I be able to walk through the garden of my own memories and feel no pain in my chest when my arm is around them in every scene? Or will the unexpected sight of them always rush through me in a gust, whistling the ghost of their laughter everywhere at once?

I don't know.

But I know that there is a monarch butterfly garden named after my grandpa in the neighborhood he used to love. I know that there is a very patient cat who endured lassoing by a tiny cowboy buried somewhere no one remembers. I know that someone received an arrangement of tiger lilies on a warm

August day years ago, and that they only lasted about a week. I know that I'm gathering things I call precious, and someday someone will swipe their fingers across the top and marvel at the dust before they carry them away. I know that it's okay to make room on my shelves. I know that snowflakes melt.

Some days I feel like I need forgiveness. Others, I am desperate for compassion. Sometimes I wake up rasping from my thirst for someone to tell me it's not in my head, and that I deserved better. On dark nights, I want someone to tell me that all of it is my fault.

The things we pack away wait for us to come back to them, unchanging while we carry on being human. We gather stories and heartbreaks, wins and losses, and we show up in garages as very different people than we were when we last decided what we thought was precious enough to save. Sometimes we find love and old friends and very cheap vibrators. Sometimes we find complicated, coiled grief.

I have started to learn how to let things go, and it has changed me into somebody new. Somebody who does not need to put reminders of the things I've lost up on my shelves, but who might need to hold on to them a little bit longer before I know what to do. I don't know who I'll be the next time I open the box with the things I felt were worth saving.

I cannot speak for anyone else, or even for who I might turn into, but for me? I'm glad I slipped all the unexpected grief into the Keep bin and tucked it away again. I'm not sure how long it will stay, but I do know that before it was painful, it was precious.

Perhaps it can be both.

Hear Me, My Love

Hear me, my love,
so I may call you when I wake
when I feel the touch of time
when I suffer that dull ache.

Hear me, my love,
the only sacred thing I savor,
so I may free you from your prison,
so I may peel away the layers.

Hear me, my love,
so I may prove to you my favor,
teeth and tongue upon you,
so I may moan under your flavor.

Hear me, my love,
so I may tell you that you've saved me
from the gnawing thing that comes at night.
You have stopped the pain from spreading,
you are my constant guiding light.

(This poem is about string cheese.)

an ode to cheese
& those born hungry

I may have been a virgin until I was twenty-nine years old,[1] but I've been fucking with cheese my whole life.

I'm talking full-fat, triple crème, aged, smoked, crumbled, nacho—you name it, I have enthusiastically consented. Even when I was but a fetus, stewin' deep with naught a functioning brain cell, I was using whatever weird biology I could to force my mother to stuff her face with fettuccine Alfredo. Would *we* like Parmesan on that? Don't ask questions you already know the answer to. Do we want to upgrade to a bufala burrata? Oh, *I don't know*, do I want to pet every dog I see? OBVIOUSLY! GOD.

I have no idea if my mother was eating soft cheese. It was the '90s, she was hypervigilant and a great mom (prenatals up the wazoo), and I'm doing A-OK, so let's all move on. I imagine if she hadn't eaten what I demanded, I would have, like, caused internal bleeding or something. We all have to make tough choices. What I'm saying is, I didn't know much as a clump of

---

1. This is true, there's more about it in another chapter.

cells,[2] but one thing was truer than the laws of nature could govern: I was, fundamentally, a bread and cheese girl. And I was born hungry.

But life isn't easy for hungry girls.[3]

Others say we want too much, we demand too much, and we expect too much. If you've been told the same, you might be hungry, too.

When we love other people, we want their approval. We want to make them proud and make them laugh, and we want them to look at us and say, "Wow, you're doing so well! Keep going!" But not everyone we love can react to us that way, because there are rules. There are certain people who are allowed to reach for the sky, and then there is everyone else. Everyone else needs to be content with the moderate success and moderate adventure yielded to them from the ones who have some imaginary claim to it all, and if they ask for more, they are to be brought back down to earth. If you end up hungry for more than other people deem your share, you are policed by your community back into an appetite appropriate for your station in life. A lot of well-meaning people end up clipping their loved ones' wings.

I learned fast that little girls aren't supposed to love decadent, full-fat, indulgent things, and we aren't supposed to crave a decadent, full-fat, indulgent life. In fact, I was taught that if I ever wanted to be accepted into a community and granted access to the exclusive club of femininity, I needed to live my life in devotion to *restriction.*

Restriction is the woman's code. We are to get the smaller plate, have the smaller serving, and not ask for seconds. We are

2. I don't actually believe that fetuses are people with sentience—I think it was pure biology. Before my neural tube was formed, these cells were pushing for cream sauce. Just evolution stuff.

3. For hungry *anyone* who isn't a very specific portion of the population.

supposed to ask, "*Is that fat-free?*" And we're supposed to say, "*Oh no, I'm fine, I'm so full! Don't worry about me!*" We are not supposed to be first in line, or to take the first plate, and we are never to take the last slice of anything. So we learn to keep ourselves from indulgence, opulence, and decadence at all costs. No matter how overstuffed it may be, we are never to take from the plate of someone who has more than their share of something we might fancy for ourselves. After all, we are not Marie Antoinette, or maybe we are, and neither of those possibilities encourage us to get a second helping.

So we learn to restrict, from the day we're born until the day that we die. Once we've sufficiently denied ourselves pleasure, we are supposed to brag about this denial to the women around us. Performing it establishes restriction as acceptable and encouraged behavior and gives the other women a blueprint for how to be. It establishes the rule and the requirements for entry. It creates a status quo and a culture that would require great effort and cost for an individual to disrupt. We are meant to posture and pose, and to speak in terms of morality when talking about food and pleasure, so we use terms like "good" and "bad" to describe foods and eating, or *not* eating. We link morality to our consumption or lack thereof. We turn our ability to deny ourselves pleasure into a declaration of personal good or evil.

"Fries or a salad?"

"Oh, no, I'm trying to be *good*. A salad please—balsamic on the side?"

There are powerful people invested in upholding this societal status quo, and part of their strategy relies on the smothering of outliers. We might not even be asking for something huge and silly when we get rejected and criticized by the ones we hope will encourage us. We may only be asking for someone to cosign our wild idea to run away to Italy and paint by the riverside or sing for euros, but one person breaking the mold and succeeding is a crack in the facade. If one outlier succeeds, someone comes after them. Soon there are so many, they are not outliers anymore. Soon, it is a valid way to live, just another option for those of us who have traditionally been given a much smaller brochure on life and its options.

The power makers cannot afford to let us choose our own unique path. So they make it costly to take more than we've been assigned, and that scares people. Suddenly, without even knowing it, the people who love us can end up working against us to keep us from growing. We tell someone important that we are dreaming of doing something indulgent, brave, and big, and they bite their nails and fret and wonder aloud, "Maybe just start a little smaller? See how that goes?"

We want someone to believe in us the way we believe in everyone else. It's hard to realize that at the big moment when you're ready to take the leap and you need your people to be cheering you on with optimism and genuine support, they might not be the ones you've built into your life so far. You can't let that quell your appetite. They don't know any better. They don't know the burn of a heart that wants more.

They might not be ready. Maybe your people are still on their way.

It's okay to be the only one who is believing in you.

I didn't know that for a very long time. I spent most of my life dreaming after things I believed, deep down, I could have— only to have the people I loved tell me that I was expecting far too much. Some of them wanted to cut me down, some of them wanted to make sure I didn't challenge their understanding of the way the world works, and some of them just wanted to keep me safe and far away from the pain of failure and loss.

No matter their reason, their opinions mattered to me. They

really mattered. Because they *knew* me and they knew what I was capable of, and they thought I was shooting too high. I was terrified of proving them right and letting them down. What if I ignored their warnings, tried, and failed? Would everyone realize I wasn't the person they thought I was? Would everyone I loved . . . leave me? If I couldn't control my hunger, they would leave, and I'd end up alone.

In a world where I'd been met with enthusiastic support for all the wild dreams I've dreamed, I think you'd be reading words written by a very different person. I might have done musical theater or gotten singing lessons and tried out for a competition show. Maybe I would have learned to scuba dive, or fly trick planes, or pull saltwater taffy. I might have pursued art and learned to paint with the oils my great-grandmother left behind. I might have snuck out, and gone to the college parties, and been in every single photo. Maybe I would have been brave enough to kiss the boys with flushed cheeks who reached up to hold my face in their hands under starlight. I might have even let the one who made me try to earn his love go before my heart got broken.

But I was too hungry and wanted too much, and everyone made sure I knew it. So I stayed small and hoped that that could keep me safe. I left the thousands of lives I could have lived untouched to walk forward on the road so many had walked before me. I would be good. I wouldn't be the sort of girl who couldn't control her appetite.

There is such a strong relationship between the way we are socialized to interact with our appetite for food and our appetites for other delicacies. Subduing our cravings for more, for richness, means we are superior. Restriction makes us better than our peers, both morally and practically, and recognized as such by more powerful people. Those who succeed are given access to places they didn't have before, are in on the joke, and are brought into more expensive rooms. And all those slobs who can't control themselves and give into their animal hunger? They aren't worthy of the higher places. They need to be corralled.

As someone who was on a diet on and off from the time I was eight years old, I can say that situating hunger for a big life onto the framework of dieting is natural and easy. When I was told I was eating too much, I ate less and was ashamed. When I was told I was asking for too much, I asked for less and was ashamed. I wonder how many of us have been subjected to this without even knowing it. I wonder how many girls who check their scales every day and count their macros religiously don't realize they are also checking the weight of their desires, measuring the nutrition of their ambition. It's just second nature. Isn't it?

So I'd chosen a diet life.

Until one day, at the flower shop where I'd been working a dead-end job for three years—uninspired and restless, but playing by the rules—my coworker and friend accidentally said the thing I'd been avoiding out loud. We had a new employee in the shop, and somehow some of the things I'd previously accomplished when I used to be hungry had come up in the get-to-know-ya chatter.

The new coworker said something like, "Wow, you've done all that?"

And my old friend said, "Yeah, she used to be a real go-getter."

She used to be a real go-getter.

Hooooooohkay. That stung.

"*Used* to be?" I repeated. She immediately realized what had come out of her mouth.

"Still is! Of course you still are! I didn't mean to say that!" But it was out, and she *had* meant it, and we both knew it. She was one of the rare people who always encouraged the hunger in others, loading seconds onto plates before they'd even cleared their first helpings. She spoke about my ambition like a long-lost friend who had gone wandering and hadn't come home.

You know what though? I'm glad she said it. It awakened something I had left buried and quiet under the dark earth of my heart. It brought back something I'd lost.

There was too much life ahead of me to be described in *used-to-bes*. In the stark light of someone else's confirmation, I realized I was very sick of playing it small. I could feel the first pricks of that burning call, like a limb coming to life after being left in a strange position for too long. My appetite was coming back.

It grew and grew. One year later, when I heard the beckoning of adventure and risk, I was hungry enough to leap. My life had changed, *I* needed to change, and I needed to be reminded of who I really was. My logic was pretty simple: Scotland was the last place I'd felt like myself, and I thought, *If I'm going to find myself again, might as well go to the last place I remember seeing me. Maybe I'll get lucky and run into an old friend.*

After all the time in my life I'd spent suffocating my ambition to stay in a safer lane, trying to secure the love and approval of people who mattered to me, and failing, I'd made a decision: *I would bet on myself.*

And fuck me, it *worked*.

Now I tell stories for a living that carry me to far-off and wonderful places. I've stopped being the first one to tell me *no*. I sing to heal my soul. I wake up when I want to. I kiss the boys who want to kiss me when I want to. I accept that I'm *alive* and that I have a healthy appetite.

Finally, I *feel like* I deserve it. I don't question if I have asked for too much, or if I have taken more than my share. That's such a milestone, isn't it? To be given something wonderful and not wonder if it's meant to be yours?

I want to ask you, Dear Reader, as a hungry little thing

who routinely eats string cheese in the middle of the night like a happy rat: Why can't you have a rich, full-fat life? Why can't you celebrate your hunger for more?

There are a lot of people you'll encounter who have already decided what you do and do not deserve based on their shallow, one-dimensional understanding of the world. People who look like X do not deserve Y. People who do X don't deserve Y. Those ideas were usually bought and paid for by the powers that be and beamed into their little heads via advertising, storytelling, movies, media, etc. The life other people think you deserve has very, very little to do with you.

So why can't you have cheese and salami for dinner? (So French, so *chic*.) Why aren't you allowed to love a lush, chocolate-nosed red wine on a Wednesday just because the feel of it in your mouth turns you into a main character, or have a four-poster bed with the downy pillows? Why can't you have a lover who always makes you finish first?[4]

On days that I feel the sharp and sudden pain of mourning the time I lost while I chose a diet life, I gently ask the grief to scooch over so it can share the space in my chest with the newer found joy and peace. Most days they live in harmony. Most days I do not question if I deserve this big, wonderful life. I have started to dream about what comes next. I try to dream unencumbered. And sure, I might end up just another falling boy with high hopes and wax wings, but shit, at least I tried.

I won't lie to you and say my path to choosing to honor my hunger for life has been without pain or failure. But I can honestly say I have been *safe*, and I have been *free*, and the hurt is

4. My editor pointed out that the majority of this paragraph is just me describing French women. Perhaps I just want everyone to adopt French Woman Food and Sex Vibes. Yes, that sounds right.

worth the feeling of finally belonging to yourself. Hunger pains, I suppose, are just part of the gig.

I found my fire in Scotland. For you, it might be somewhere entirely different. I'm very lucky and privileged for things to have gone the way they have in my life, and not everyone could do things like that. That's unfair. I wish with my whole heart that everyone could have exactly what they felt they needed to find their quickest path to peace.

But we all have something that calls us: a thing to do, or a way to be, or a place to go. There is something that beckons, from deep in the dark corners of our souls where we never draw the curtains and let the sun in, that asks us to feed the hunger for life. To leave the predictable, sturdy table where we eat a "reasonable" amount and nothing more, and to open a brand-new door. It beckons us to *change*.

Maybe you'll start a new career later in life just because you've always wanted to try it. Maybe I'll see you giving speeches to rooms full of important people, see you driving with the top down on a winding road, see you burning a recipe you decided to try for the first time and laughing while you frantically fan the smoke. I hope you move to the new place, or dye your hair the new color, or find new friends who like to Rollerblade on Sundays, too. Perhaps you'll be walking down the aisle to your third husband, all smiles and joy because he makes you happy, with only flowers and no regret cradled in your arms.

Your change might not be as drastic as the person's next to you. Your hunger might look different. You might want to learn to crochet, or to move to a place with evergreens, or to adopt a senior cat. No one can tell you what your adventure is supposed to look like, but I do know one thing:

There is too much life ahead of all of us to be described in *used-to-bes*. I pray we are all hungry until the day we die. I pray we never run out of delicious new things to fill up our plates with and try. After all, we only have the one life. We only have the one chance.

So fuck fat-free.

It's a decadent, indulgent life from here on out.

we deserve better supervillains than a dude named jeff

Billionaires are garbage. The capitalist circle jerk that lauds them as heroes is a dirty little farce. It's so unethical for the tiniest speck of the globe's people to be *hoarding*[1] the money and resources that an entire half of the human population need to *literally just survive*. It's more money than they could spend in a lifetime. It's more money than they could spend in a hundred lifetimes. Meanwhile, there are people who have never done a goddamn thing but show up and work hard and be kind and honest who are getting robbed of their *one* life because they can't afford to survive it.

Fuck billionaires.

But if I'm being entirely honest, the above is only half the reason I can't stand them. The other half of me—the half that is barely bottled chaos and gets itchy without drama—is just very, very disappointed. Billionaires are real-life supervillains,[2] *so where*

---

1. Like a little troll with treasures, or a dragon in a mountain but way balder, or the asshole who bought all the toilet paper during April of 2020 and left you wiping your sweet tuchus with scratchy lawn weeds.
2. Stealing from the needy and burning the planet down while you build an escape rocket ship makes you a supervillain. Shut up.

is the fucking fanfare, you nutless sacks? You have the resources to go full Bad Guy. Deliver a crushing speech about your supremacy over the peons of Manhattan from a hovercraft! Laugh into a megaphone that you've spent five million dollars developing so they can hear you in Brooklyn! Challenge a police horse to a race while wearing a jetpack! Declare sewer rats a sacred animal that everyone else must kiss on the mouth or be put to death! Do you not understand what you have at your fingertips?

You could hire Gwyneth Paltrow as your personal life coach and force everyone to buy the vagina candle from Goop. You could be draped in custom velvet *lewks*, with feathered headpieces and fitted chain mail, or you could have all your Zoom meetings from the back of a giant black stallion named Lord Licorice.

You have the entire world in your pocket, all cozy, pressed up against your butt, from the actual money to the global leaders you paid for, and the best you can do is build a rocket shaped like a ding-dong to dick-tickle outer space? Like, you really just-the-tipped it? You're telling me that's the height of the creative ceiling in there? A blue canvas onesie and a horny cowboy hat?

I refuse to accept this. If we are going to be forced to endure the reality of crumbling late-stage capitalism, collapsing into the cavern opened by the wealth divide that only grows wider and gains sharper teeth by the day, then we should *at least* get a good villain out of it. We should at least get some fucking entertainment to go along with the bottomless dread.

I'm underwhelmed, and I'm not the only one. I've been chatting with Outer Space, and she's so unimpressed with your performance after you barely got in there. I bet you thought she'd nickname you something like "Earth Daddy"' in the group chat. But guess what, dude? You're exclusively known to all the hot celestial bodies as "the Real Lil' Dipper." I hope that brings you shame, you Lil' Dip.

For fun, let's do an exercise to keep our minds sharp, like sudoku or a quick crossword. Close your eyes, take a deep breath, and picture the world if a group of overworked and under-recognized women suddenly swapped lives with the Billionaire Boys Club. What would be different? What would be better? If my girls and I had that much money at our disposal *and* the total lack of conscience that seems to afflict our limp Lex Luthors, we'd be hitting Villain Chic so fucking hard. After all, *we* know what it's like to have to do more than the bare minimum for praise and power, am I right?

Personally, I'd channel a combo of Ursula,[3] Yzma,[4] and Saint Olga,[5] and it wouldn't stop there. If I know my gal pals (which I do), there would be more than one sweaty man who was once a CEO now living life as a pool boy. Just endless days in our ridiculous backyards wearing, like, a feathered boa and a glitter thong and refreshing our martinis when we ring a little bell. The stock market definitely wouldn't be a thing. We'd barter and trade for pretty seashells and rare cheeses and bedazzled javelins. "Cryptocurrency" would just be what we call the fake money we pay men for their labor, and it would only be composed of tangible things like buttons and old sticks of gum we find in the purgatory of our purses. "But I'm rich!! I trade in crypto!" Oh yeah, big boy? Show me the buttons, then. *Show me the fucking buttons.*

---

3. *The Little Mermaid* totally underappreciated this epic baddie and fat icon. She has pet eels with kitschy little names. I love pets with kitschy little names.

4. Saggy-boobed, evening-dressed visionary queen in *The Emperor's New Groove* with eyelashes reaching the heavens and a himbo boyfriend. She's a chemist and an engineer. We love a woman in STEM.

5. A real woman who sought revenge on the people who murdered her husband by saying she'd marry their ruler if he gave her the pet birds from every household. She sent them back to their nests with burning embers tied to their feet, and burned their city down. You can't tell Olga shit.

We'd make saying "Women are *crazy*" punishable by death, or even better, banishment to Broke Boys Island where offenders have nothing but three coconuts and other naked dudes blistering in the sun to stare at. If girls got to be the unhinged and obscenely wealthy supervillains, you bet your overworked ass there'd be fashion, there'd be drama, there'd be showstopping musical numbers à la *Chicago*. (We'd make the pool boys dance.)

What I'm saying is, what if you gave the gals the chance to ruin the planet with our greed? To run wild and devour the earth in sick cash grabs for the sake of our vanity then escape to outer space to watch the flames from somewhere safe, draped in blood-colored velvet capes and shit? The world would burn far more fabulously. After all, everyone loves a woman in red.

So Billi-Boys, if you're going to continue to be a collection of the most evil men to ever walk the planet, I hope you can at least step up the production value of this horror show. I want to be on the edge of my seat. I want to be vividly aware that my life is in the hands of a couple of egomaniacs who get to choose for all of humanity. I want to be constantly refreshing my phone, waiting for the tweet that says two of you are having a whip-it-out-and-measure-it contest again, and one of you resurrected a T. rex to bring to the fight. Jurassic Park–level recklessness is the bottom line. If you're not peeling mosquitoes out of amber to vex your enemies and prove once and for all that everyone, even time, is your bitch, you're not doing enough. You're just not doing enough.

We are *not* entertained. We are just exasperated and Googling the French Revolution a lot more frequently these days. So I'd suggest rising above the bare minimum for once.

It's showtime!

Not Nice

I'm not nice,
I'm kind—

That's different.

Kindness demands bite
sometimes.

There may be people with bleeding hands
who will tell you that I'm *mean*, but

I'm not mean,
I'm kind—

That's different.

intimidating women
& fear boners

There is a certain type of man who tends to get a funny little feeling around a certain type of woman, and they don't like the funny feeling at all. They start to scrunch up their eyebrows, squint their eyes, and tap their little feet. They are full of swirling emotions and itchy in their heads. They are uncomfy, but they don't know why, so they put their keen, penetrating minds to the test. They ask themselves some questions.

Why am I suddenly feeling like this lady needs to shut the fuck up? Like I need to do something to express my He-Man power? Why am I suddenly compelled to mention that she is an icy, old witch who I would never have sex with? And also, why do I have a boner?

These types of men specialize in man-logicing their way to uninspired conclusions about women but are far too emotional to draw conclusions about *themselves*. All that gorgeous brainpower crunches the numbers and analyzes the facts and does its very manly dance to spit out an explanation for their reaction. Those churlish imps puff out their chests and prepare to deliver the diagnosis:

They wield unruly, inexplicable boners (to which they will

never admit) for one reason and one reason only: *the woman in question is very intimidating.*

I've heard it so many times.

It makes me tired because I'm not intimidating. They are *intimidated*. That's very different.

When I'm getting ready for a date, I do pretty normal things. I take too long on my hair and struggle to get the perfect wing on my eyeliner. I try on a few outfits before I settle on something familiar and comfortable. I make sure I smell good.

What I *don't* do is stare at myself in the mirror while I smear football player face shit under my eyes, and bark, "INTIMIDATE MEN! LONG LIVE THE FEMINIST AGENDA!" I don't get myself into the headspace of rugby players heading into a championship match, ready to knock out some teeth or die trying. I don't think about what outfits best say, "I have a bigger dick than you." I don't consider wearing an old-timey revolver on my belt so they know, from the instant they bust through the swinging door of the saloon we've agreed to have a sad cocktail in, that I have the fastest hands in the fucking West, bub.

Yet I am constantly accused of being SO intimidating. Too smart! Too witty! Too beautiful in person! He didn't expect that! Like, woah, I'm really pretty!

In the face of all my qualities, he is feeling small and unimpressive, and that's my fault. I did it on purpose, icy bitch that I am! He has an awkward erection fed by his fear and lust because I am a wicked little snake charmer, and that has nothing to do with him. So *hmph!*

This sort of man feeling intimidated by women's basic presence and sense of self is a man problem. Everyone encounters people who are better than them at things every single day. Women aren't intimidating just because they are smarter, faster, and better than them. They *feel* intimidated because they have a deep-seated belief that women are worse than them at everything that matters.[1] When confronted with a woman who challenges that belief, they experience a wave of confusing emotions and reactions, and they blame it on anybody but themselves.

Shitty men blaming women for their behaviors is a long-respected practice with this particular breed. While the accusation of intimidation is ridiculous, it's not the most nefarious manifestation of this manipulation tactic.

When I was a teenager involved in the Christian church, we were routinely taught that our choice of clothing was directly responsible for how often our Brothers in Christ, uh, *handled* their Staff of Moses. Once, when I was about seventeen, the other girls and I were called into the youth pastor's office and sat down for a Very Serious Chat. We were informed that leadership had been alerted to photos of us in various styles of bathing attire at the beach posted on our Facebook pages. A perfectly choreographed Heavy Pause and a Searching Gaze were employed against us. When we didn't immediately volunteer our regret at being uncouth cultists in servitude to Hester Prynne, we were *informed* that we were guilty of causing our brothers to stumble. Actually, it was one brother in particular—just a clumsy little guy who had recently confessed to being forced into spiritual servitude with the constant choking of Satan's chicken.[2] When pressed for details about what, in particular, was luring the poor boy into the lotion and tissue aisle again and again, he pointed one sticky finger at *us*. It was *our fault* for having been in bathing suits at the beach, like, that one time. *And* putting it on the internet, all skanky style. What was he to do? What was he to think? How was his lil' winkie, with all

---

1. This is, again, about a certain type of man.
2. Ah!! How did my hand get in my pants?! WHAT WITCHCRAFT!?

the self-control of a starving dog presented with filet mignon, *supposed* to react? He was just a boy, and we were practically turning his brain into a demonic titty bar from which there was no escape. He was spiritually covered in stripper glitter, and that shit just wouldn't come off.[3]

Even if you've never had the pleasure of being slut-shamed in the name of Jesus, I'd bet that almost every woman and non-cis man reading this book was kept from wearing clothes in school that were comfortable for the summer heat. After all, if the boys realize you have skin on your shoulders or knees, it would be catastrophic. Their brains would melt, and they would all liter-ally forget how to do math. They would become small scuttling beetles who can do nothing but follow their little beetle brains, and then the world would collapse because we wouldn't have any more engineers.[4] If girls came to school with spaghetti straps, we wouldn't have a single usable bridge or road, or any drone strike technology. The country's infrastructure would crumble and we'd be invaded in a land war. Those deeply immoral shoul-ders would single-handedly be responsible for the downfall of the United States.

This is, of course, just one mutation of the same general argument that has been employed to excuse the misogynistic behavior of cis men for eons. *Because girls are X, boys have no option but to be Y.* Girls are responsible for the behavior of boys. Women are responsible for the behavior of men.[5] Smart women who have visible knee skin and are gainfully employed are *very intimidating.* That's why they're *still* single, you know.

I can't help but wonder if those who believe in this way of

3. Unlike him, whose constant getting off was the reason we were all here.
4. *Girls* can't be engineers, duh.
5. Girls are also held responsible for the behavior of grown fucking men.

the world can see the deep flaw in their argument. Beyond the glaringly obvious and disgusting bits, isn't arguing that men are literally incapable of choosing their own thoughts and behaviors . . . reductive? Aren't you being a little anti-man by arguing that they are all such unthinking, prehistoric gym socks that they can't stop their weens from just, like, ending up in someone accidentally? Isn't positing that they're rocking nothing more than the shriveled dingle-brain of their Neanderthal cousins sloshing around in the ol' noggin a distinctly man-hating take?

But I digress.

While it may seem like the people calling for the end of intimidating women are mindlessly making their way through life without much impact or purpose, it is, overall, a very strategic method of control. Intimidating is a word used intentionally. Intimidating people are big, burly, bulky, and carry a threat of violence. Intimidating people are, in other words, *masculine*.[6] Masculine is a critical insult in the effort to control and monitor the movements of women.

Intimidation boners aside, it's well understood that masculine women are not desirable to this nasty sort of man, but they do threaten their power. We are not supposed to try to step upward on the ladder and poke our little heads through the barrier between femininity and masculinity. Should a woman find herself in that realm by accident, she is reminded right away that she has been stripped of her value and is at dire risk of dying alone without anyone to protect her. (*You're just too intimidating, sweetie. Try smiling more!*) Should a woman try to enter the realm of masculinity on purpose, she is usually met with violence. Gay cis men who express femininity are met with violence. Trans people are just met with violence no matter what,

---

6. By traditional and widely socially accepted definitions.

as their very existence demonstrates that the boundary between masculine and feminine is constructed and can be destroyed. These cis men protect masculinity with violence, because they will protect their unearned power at any cost.[7]

It is not only physical appearance that draws the ire. Non-cis men exhibiting traits like intelligence, self-respect, eloquence, ambition, humor, independence, leadership, directness, confidence, and success pose a threat, too. People like this are the ones who earn the title: INTIMIDATING!

The threat of being branded intimidating is meant to elicit a specific response. We are supposed to understand that to be a masculine woman is to accept being unloved and unwanted; it is a threat of loss of resources and the promise of physical danger. We are meant to immediately reconsider our behavior and presentation, identify where we are going too far or taking up too much room, and adjust, so that we can ensure our safety. We are supposed to instantly shrink down to accommodate the insecurity of the cis men in the room. If we don't, we are branded as someone who should be thrown out and left in the cold, forever separated from the power and safety that being partnered with a man can afford us.

Fuck that, though. Am I right?

If you've ever been told that you're "too intimidating" for doing anything short of personally tattooing barbed wire on your own meaty weight-lifter thigh in the back of a van while, stone-faced, you drink the smokiest whisky straight from the bottle and make unyielding eye contact with your intimidation-accuser before growling, "What are you lookin' at, Baby Face?" you have been lied to. There is a huge difference between being a person with self-esteem and self-respect, and

7. Also, fuck TERFs.

being someone who walks around trying to poke indiscriminate men in the chest *real hard* until they cry.[8]

Intimidating is not an insult. It's more of a badge of honor. Each time we refuse to react the way they want us to, we reduce the potency of the tactic. So go forth, smart, funny, honest people. Go forth and carry all your wonders with you into every first date. Turn every head in the place. Sit at the bar and order something tall and strong. If your date ends up being a bit disappointing, make the hot bartender laugh. Flirt until the hot bartender starts saying things like, "It's on the house." Take the hot bartender home.

Carry on being the sort of person whose very presence inspires a confused, emotional, scared-chihuahua erection. May we always challenge reductive tales of who is allowed to be what. May we laugh loudly, may we speak surely, and may we tattoo our own thighs in the back of a van. May we forever inspire baffling fear boners in the weaker sort.

---

8. If you're super *into* making men cry, I see you. You probably make great money. But that's *different* and you know it.

Bitter Ink

I'm so glad it was *you* who broke *my* heart.
Careless of you, really. You know I write the hell out of pain.

rejection, failure
& the end of the world[1]

I wish you could have seen me when I was in junior high.

I was smearing body glitter I'd won at Chuck E. Cheese all over my chest, face, and arms and calling it fashion.[2] My makeup routine was slathering a hauntingly orange foundation that was advertised as "whipped mousse" in a flat, thick layer over my greasy face, and caking on whatever eyeshadow I could finger out of the only compact I owned—which was pretty much blacks and blues, so I looked perpetually bruised. My dagger-straight eyelashes were (and still are) less like the fluttering beauties of a wide-eyed Disney Princess and more like a thin line of angry little toothpicks, hissing at anything threatening to lengthen or curl them. I dressed them up anyway, with a swipe of turquoise mascara that smelled like sugar cookies.

The photos of me from that time in my life look like the

---

1. While this may sound like a preteen rom-com, the following is, to the best of my recollection, a true fucking story.

2. In hindsight, the Chuck E. Cheese body glitter that you won for dominating at Skee-Ball was probably off-brand lube with shards of real glass and blue food coloring, which could explain a lot about who I turned into as an adult.

Michelin Man and a bottle of vegetable oil had a daughter who hadn't learned about conditioner yet, and who dreamed of running away to the circus. Deep in the throes of puberty, that strange little gremlin was one part blazing insecurity, one part raging god complex, and one hundred percent besotted with *boys*.

I went to great lengths to be noticed by them. There was Cameron, who I tried to impress by jumping over a desk (*boys love sporty girls*), and ended up with my skirt over my head and my *SpongeBob* undies on display. Then Nelson, for whom I started using black eyeliner on my waterline so poorly that I looked pink-eye-esqe, because he was, like, *emo*. And there was Peter, who I tried to send a love poem to over AOL Instant Messenger the day he moved away, only to find I didn't have his real AIM name.[3]

But all paled in comparison to Justin Nichols, who had the slight build of a boy not-yet-hit-puberty, a perfect head of blond hair that my parents said looked like a stormtrooper helmet he couldn't take off, and a scar barely cutting a slit through his eyebrow. Justin was brand new to me since he'd gone to another elementary school, and since I'd cycled through crushes on every boy twice by then, fresh meat was beguiling. Sure, we had never *really* talked, and he was shorter than me, and he weighed as much as a hungry rescue cat and a handful of Funyuns, but I was in love with him.

It was almost Bring Your Walkman to School Day, and most of us were rocking a mini-CD player and a zip-up case full of compact discs that we treated like dragon's gold. I took inventory of my CD stash, and I was struck by a *genius* idea. I knew

---

3. Peter and I are still in touch. He recently learned of the mishap with the AIM name and the lost love poem, and he declared, "I want that poem more than I've wanted anything in my entire life." He insists that the only two lines I remember should be inscribed on our wedding bands, should we ever marry. I insist that I will only let that happen if we also inscribe the small, rudimentary emoji of a crying chicken I used as punctuation.

exactly three things about Justin Nichols: (1) He played . . . a sport of some kind, (2) his favorite band was the Foo Fighters, and (3) he was the love of my life. So the day before Bring Your Walkman to School Day, I begged my mom to take me to the CD store, and I bought the first Foo Fighters album I saw, checked my Walkman's batteries, and got to scheming.

Justin and I had one class together, and it was set up *just right* for my expert level of lovespionage. Miss Heller's English class had the seats arranged in a U shape so that some students would be facing each other across the large gap in the middle of the room. I had a direct line of sight to my sexy bird-boned prey, and I came to school that day with the mind, the heart, and the playlist of a hunter.

Miss Heller was a Very Cool Teacher, so she had planned a silent reading and work block for the second half of class for us to enjoy the novelty. I pulled out my Walkman, a yellow-and-black number made bulky with nonskip tech, turned the volume all the way up, and pressed Play. A gravelly voice and guitar poured through the flimsy headphones I'd stolen from an airplane the summer before. It was deafening in the clinical sense, but love conquers all. Justin Nichols *would* hear the sweet siren song of Dave Grohl drifting across the classroom, and Justin Nichols *would* look my way. Our eyes would lock—mine from under my turquoise lashes, his from under his golden fringe—and something urgent and foreverish would pass between us. Soulmates, that's what we were. And he would know it, just as soon as he recognized "Best of You" emanating from my effortless person across the classroom.

I was looking down, playing it cool while I waited for the inevitable meet-cute, when it finally happened—a tap on my desk, and my heart leaped into my chest. *He was here, tapping on my desk.* All I had to do was look up, coquettish as eff, and we'd be Elizabeth and Fitzwilliaming this shit until we died. Our epic love story would be engraved onto our marble mausoleums, probably. I took a quick breath, arranged my features into the most *come-hither* expression a pudgy tween with braces possibly could, and flicked my eyes up to where his should have been.

Breasts. I was staring at breasts—in a sensible, modest, V-neck sweater. The kind a teacher might wear.

It was not Justin tapping on my desk to tell me this was the beginning of the rest of our lives. It was Miss Heller, and I was still staring at her breasts in abject horror as her long, willowy arms crossed over them in obvious annoyance and fire leaped to my face.

She mimed for me to take my headphones off.

I took them off, gulped, and raised my gaze to her guillotine eyes.

Eyes she narrowed like she was sharpening a blade. "I've been asking you to turn that down for *an entire sixty seconds.*"

Do you know how long sixty seconds is, Dear Reader? How long it *really* is—in a silent room, full of churlish preteens, all staring at a huge black-and-white clock on the wall while the vindictive, bright-red second hand loudly ticks its way sixty times in a circle? Sixty seconds as the only adult in the room repeats, "Turn that down," over and over until you want to perish under the collective scrutiny of peers and authority figures alike?

It's a long fucking time, okay?

I choked, "Sorry, Miss Heller."

She tapped a toe[4] until I turned the music all the way down, then she spun on the spot and began to click-clack her way back to the front, punctuating the thick silence with her heeled retreat.

With the same courage I'm sure Joan of Arc or William

---

4. I believe, if I recall, she was suppressing a smile and wearing very fabulous shoes.

Wallace donned as they stepped into their last moments, I dropped my eyes to meet my classmates.

Every. Single. Person. Was. Staring. But I only cared about *one.*

The thing about being in love when you're twelve years old is that you can't *actually* make eye contact with the person you're in love with—that's the rule. If they *see* you *seeing* them, it is the bona fide end of the world. You can be in love and you can fill diaries with the names of your future children, but getting caught staring means you've just been emotionally pantsed in the emotional quad at emotional lunch.

So I had to play it cool. I choked back the rising tide of *ef-feffeff* in my chest and very casually went back to working on my homework, insisting on normalcy. And it worked—I felt the cling film of attention start to peel up at the edges as the classroom of oily preteens lost interest. When I felt like I could breathe without an inhaler again, I gathered my courage and risked a glance at Justin Nichols.

He was still staring. His face was inscrutable, but that could be good. Darcy looked at Elizabeth that way, and all the while behind that studied mask he was planning to confess that he loved her. (*Most ardently.*) Justin was staring at me without expression because he was plotting which countryside hill he'd confess his love to me on next time it rained, or something. Our story had just begun.

When my mom asked me how school was, I had to fight the urge to shout that it was the best day of my life. Later that night, I sat at her desktop computer, dreamily floating on a cloud of possibility and thinking about where Justin and I would honeymoon while I updated my away message with bRb and *~*, when the telltale sound of an AIM message shot through my fantasy. My heart sped up. I read it.

"hey"

That "*hey*" submerged me in a bath of ice water while my stomach fell out of my butthole.

The message was from *Matt Flanders*.

Matt Flanders was Justin Nichols's best friend.

Matt Flanders had never messaged me before, and he'd obviously been sent by Justin.

That was the most magical "hey" that had ever been *hey*-ed. It was a "hey" that would launch a thousand ships, quell a thousand wars, and win a thousand hearts.

I wrote back "*sup?*"

And I waited.

And waited.

Oh my god, what was he typing? No, I knew what he was typing. He was about to tell me Justin was in love with me. He was going to ask if I liked Justin too, check *yes* or *no* style.

ping!

"*do u lyk Justin Nichols?*"

Hyperventilating. Avril Lavigne's "My Happy Ending" played in the background while I typed, and erased, and typed, and erased like I was composing a Shakespearean sonnet on the fly. I was about to press Send on "*y? Duz he lyk me?*" when another *ping* stopped me—

"*were pretty sure lyk half the gurlz in our grade lyk him so were tryin to count them all*"

Wait . . . what? Half the girls like him?

ping!

"*so far itz lyk 28 gurlz or sumthin*"

I'm sorry . . . what!?

Matt Flanders wasn't messaging me because Justin Nichols had heard the Foo Fighters damaging my eardrums and become enraptured, it was because he had so many options he literally had to tally them.

I wasn't a number, I was soulmate material! How could he not *know* that? In that instant, I decided I didn't like Justin Nichols, or his ugly, lank hair anymore. I buried our imaginary children in tiny little caskets in my head and typed,

"thatz so dumb."

I DID NOT like Justin Needs-A-Haircut Nichols, and now everybody, including Matt Freakin' Flanders, knew it. Good. There could be no doub—

ping!

"so thatz a yes"

Effeffeff

I was prepared to tell him I loved him as long as I knew he loved me too. But Justin was about to find out about my über-embarrassing, world-ending, *unrequited* crush. Like, is there anything worse, in the entire scope of the human experience, than your middle school crush who absolutely does not *like*-like you, finding out that you absolutely do *like*-like him?

No, there is not.

My entire life was about to collapse. I mean, what even happens when the boy you're absolutely in love with who should NEVER cut his perfect hair finds out you're doodling his name in your notebook? All I knew was that I couldn't survive it. That level of shame? That level of embarrassment? That level of failure? You never come back from that. Death was upon me. I was about to die, and I'd never even seen my own smile without braces or owned a hair straightener. My idea of beauty was rubbing Chuck E. Cheese lube-glitter into my sweaty crevices before trucking it to PE, and I WAS ABOUT TO DIE.

I typed feverishly, *"nuh uh, thatz a lie Matt."* Then to really ice that cake I added, *"dont b so st00pid"*

I'll admit it wasn't my best self telling Matt Flanders he was st00pid with two zeros for *o*'s, but I was desperate.

I was deciding what sort of torture I was going to threaten Matt Freakin' Flanders with if he told Justin about my secret shame, when I heard the most bone-chilling thing I'd ever heard in my twelve years on Earth—a door creaking closed and slamming. Matt Flanders had signed off of AIM.[5]

effeffeff

But what was there to do? The next day I slunk through the hallways of that cursed, loveless land like a hunted animal, avoiding the fallout of my burning, reckless loins at all costs. What if Matt told him already? What if Justin took one look at me and projectile vomited into some poor band geek's locker? What if, Goddess Hilary Duff forbid it, he saw me and, like . . . *laughed or something?*

I ducked into the bathroom to hide. It was full of other girls, which wasn't great, but it was better than running into the boy who'd broken my heart via his best friend via AIM only hours before. I got into a stall and collapsed, breathing deeply for the first time all day, when I heard the voices that made my blood run cold. There weren't just "other girls" in the bathroom—they were the *popular girls*—the ones who hung out with Justin Nichols. They paused a moment—listening at the door of the stall I was trying to disappear in—then the air erupted in giggles.

eff.

I darted out of the bathroom, looking over my shoulder and desperate to escape the acute pain of middle school girls giggling at your expense. I took a corner a little fast in my attempt to disappear, and I slammed directly into Justin Perfect-Hair Nichols.

Fuck.

He dropped something as the bulk of my tater-tot-fed-form collided with his hollow bones.

---

5. If you are of the age of AIMers . . . you heard it just now, didn't you?

"Sorry!" I yelped, and I reached down to pick up what he'd dropped. His friends were around him in a circle looking stunned as I lifted up a small notebook, open to a page covered in scratchy boy-writing. It looked like the second half of a list, started on the page before, too long to be contained on one measly sheet:

26. *Nikki*

27. *Lauren*

28. *Kylie*

29. *Devrie*

Devrie.

This was *the* list, and my name was on it. I was number twenty-nine.

For the second time in two days, I made painful eye contact with Justin Nichols. We were maybe a foot apart. If my life had been a movie, and I had been a different girl, it would have been the moment that the sound cut out, our eyes locked, and our hands grasped the small offering between us. The camera might start to pan in a slow circle, blurring out the sidekick boys behind us while romantic music swelled from an unseen piano and our breath caught in our throats. We would be in an infinite moment, just the two of us, as the many things that had mattered moments before became irrelevant in the face of our once-in-a-lifetime kind of connection.

But it wasn't a movie. It was me, and it was *my* life, so instead when our eyes locked and his hand closed around that useless little no-good list, I barked, "I DO NOT like you like *that*, Justin. Cross my name OUT!" And it was very obvious that I was about to cry.

His friends erupted in snickering laughter as the heat sprung to my cheeks. It took me a second to realize that the only person *not* laughing at me and my pathetic attempt to salvage my dignity from the dumpster fire that was my useless little no-good life, was Justin.

He held my gaze one beat too long, and the corner of his perfect crooked mouth twitched. His eyebrow, slit by that secret scar, lifted just a tiny bit, but it didn't feel like he was mocking me. He wasn't mad. Why was he acting like this was *fun?*

Meanwhile, my body was a nuclear reactor midmelt-down—a trillion swirling particles of embarrassment and shame, of love and lust and wishing-I-could-be-anywhere-but-there ready to blow.

And why was he looking at me like that?

Justin slowly and gently pulled the list from my hand without looking away. In the riot of laughter around us, he leaned the smallest bit toward me. I flinched, but he didn't recoil.

Then Justin Nichols whispered so that his friend couldn't hear, "*Okay, but . . . it's okay if you do. It's really not a big deal.*"

Justin spun on his heels to face his friends with a look I couldn't see, and they quickly fell silent. Then he walked away from me to go to his next class, and every one of those boys followed.

I was left standing alone in a hallway growing more anemic by the second as kids streamed through classroom doors to beat the bell that would prove them truant. My hands were shaking.

Justin Nichols knew I was in love with him.

The bell rang. The first tear fell.

I'd just been laughed at by a bunch of popular kids.

I drew in one unsteady breath.

Justin Nichols knew I was in love with him, and he didn't love me . . . but he didn't hate me.

When I look back now, do you know what I see?

I see me—not a movie star but a typical, smitten girl—and a perfect-haired boy, with my heart suspended between us. As I think about what I thought would be the worst thing that ever happened to me, all I can see is my greatest fear transform from a roaring wave into a gentle splash at my feet.

The love of my life didn't like me back, and the world definitely *did not end.*

Even though I had failed, been rejected, and was left feeling as bruised as my eyeshadow cocktail made me look, the world was still spinning. I was still spinning in it.

Life moves on, even when you were so sure that it wouldn't.

But I was still a middle schooler, not fucking Gandhi, so it took me a while to really embrace that lesson or see it for what it was. I was still afraid of failure and falling short, so I continued to spend years shrinking down my world to make sure I never found myself somewhere I might slip and fail. How many roads have I been called down by my heart, only to stop myself at the beginning? How many of my soul's desires did I yank out of my chest at the root, because the wager for happiness was loss?

Eventually, when all those failures never happened but I was still unhappy, I had to confront the bare truth of my life. And the truth was this:

Rejection and failure never made my world stop spinning . . . *but I had.*

My fear of them had led me to stop life from growing and taking on the shape it was trying to take. I froze the orbit of my own little planet, reversing it and tilting it and finding a new axis, trying to stop it from spiraling into something that felt out of control. I was afraid of the end of the world, and I was sure that failure would bring it on. All the while, I was the one who made the world stop spinning again, and again, and again.

I am convinced that failure and rejection only hurt so badly because we fear them so greatly. We give them the power to confirm that we are unlovable or unworthy. We sacrifice so much of our lives, our choices and chances and big bets, *avoiding* failure and rejection—so when they catch up to us, because they always do, the very human experience feels like a failure all on its own. It feels like we've sacrificed for nothing. It confirms that we can't get anything right.

So now I try to think of failure and rejection as passing visitors who come when it's right for me and go when it's right for me. I don't try to ward them away from my heart, and I don't seek them out, but I respect them for what they are. And though their visit can be painful, I know that when they come to rest their head in my home, I will be better for knowing them in the morning. I try to think of failure and rejection as a blessing. They are proof of a life explored.

I mean, if middle school me—with my knotted hair and Bozo makeup and braces—can survive the cutest boy in school knowing I was in love with him when he didn't like me *like that* at all, there's not a goddamn thing someone like *you* can't accomplish. You've got a lot more going for you than middle school me. You're hot already, and you probably know how to brush your hair. You can just Google whatever music video you want, and your mom can't even ground you after she walks into her office to play mah-jongg and instead finds your nose pressed against the computer screen while Nelly's "Hot in Herre" writhes around underneath it. You can try, and you can fail, and you can tell someone you love them and risk it all—and you will still be okay in the morning. The world will keep spinning, and you'll still be in it. You will still be standing.

The fear of failure and rejection shouldn't be allowed to bring so many early endings to your one, magical world. We don't have to be afraid of being human.

Whisky Girl

I've always wanted to be a Whisky Girl—
to sip an old-fashioned
and kiss the melting moon into your mouth
above the New York City skyline—

so that long after I'd left,
your young lovers' breath
would barrel age you twelve years
to that moment in time:

to the smoke on your tongue,
to my prints on the glass,
to the spreading warmth of the two-fingered night.
And while the peat-earth eclipse stole the last of the light

you would reach for me in the dark, then,
wouldn't you?

Wouldn't you?

But you know I drink gin
or vodka
or wine.

Fuck.

I know you love a Whisky Girl,
and you know I can't stomach it, no matter what I try.

everything i learned from being in love

1. You can fall in love for the first time in an instant, on a Tuesday, when you are very unprepared.
2. You can try everything to shake the feeling, but sometimes love is an unkind companion, so it will not leave your side, no matter how you beg.
3. You can be in love with someone who has never been your boyfriend.
4. He can be in love with you too.
5. He can be in love with you and still not want to be with you.
6. He will still expect you to answer all of his calls.
7. You will be uncomfortably aware of the blood in your body while the one you love kisses many other people, but you will survive every time.
8. You will seek out the love you believe you deserve, but you won't know you deserve better until you're in too deep.
9. Nothing will ever hurt the same way as your first broken heart.
10. You will learn the term Emotional Girlfriend, and you

will finally make sense of the years of scar tissue no one has believed is there.

11. You will learn to forgive yourself for what you gave up when you hoped you could trade for love.

12. Time and Distance are your two greatest friends for forgetting what you have lost.

13. One day you will wake up and realize that you cannot remember the exact shade of blue of his eyes, and it will barely sting at all.

14. Love should not cost you the health of your only gentle heart.

notes from an amateur anthropologist: tinder

Field Notes: June, a.k.a. "Hot Girl Summer"
Territory: Dating app known as "Tinder"
Time in Field: This purgatory is endless.

<u>Observations:</u>

The wilds of Tinder have long mystified the modern world. It is a place of pure instinct, of pure desire. A place of survival where not everyone survives. I cannot recall how I got here, or even when. I have forgotten what the world is like on the outside. My only solace is the hope that my work here will not be in vain.

I have focused my studies on the cis-straight menfolk[1] in this godforsaken wasteland. My observations of the outside world indicate that the expectation for one potential partner to change aspects about themselves in order to secure a mate

---

1. Referred to as "men" from here on out, but not referring to trans men, who are also men but generally less problematic.

disproportionately falls on the potential partners of men. They are told they need to lose weight, gain weight, be quiet, be confident, be sexy, be virginal, be successful, be submissive, be a mother, be a cool girl, be rich, be dependent, be mysterious, be transparent—the list goes on and on. Rarely is the burden of change demanded of men, unless it is in service to a larger narrative of patriarchy, like being more muscular, dominant, and dangerous. The *actual* desires of men's potential partners are much less commonly represented in conversations of what makes someone worthy of being chosen by another, despite it being the obvious way for the lonely menfolk to become a desirable partner. Thus, my studies focus on the behavior of those very men and the potential areas for change that would benefit them greatly.

The following are my observations regarding the bizarre behavior they display in hopes of finding a female[2] mate, which are often at odds with what I know the female population finds desirable. I hope my time lost to the study of this foul place will guide those unfortunate souls lured here by the promise of true love to a more attractive profile.

I do not expect the wild Fuckboy[3] to read these notes and change a single thing. Rather, I hope that his contemporaries—soft-hearted men who earnestly seek love and companionship—can use this as a road map to a much better way of presenting themselves online. To model the wild Fuckboy

---

2. I speak from my own perspective, but there are likely non-female-identifying folk who feel the same way, or who have their own items to add to this list! Take it and run, friends!

3. The Wild Fuckboy is an invasive species, razing the land and leaving nothing behind but destruction, despair, and bad examples of connection.

is to doom oneself to certain rejection. The women no longer respond to being sought after like prey—they have been hunted for eons, and they have evolved to survive. They can sense a Fuckboy approaching from miles off.

Those men planning to get close enough to a wild woman to find happiness mustn't carry the Fuckboy stench. To escape the vile wafting and increase chances of finding love, one must avoid the following at all costs:

1. The Bitches Love Fishes Philosophy

There are an extraordinary number of men who rely on a photo of them holding a dead fish aloft to secure them a mate. I cannot say for certain what has led them to believe this is a winning strategy. Do they think that they are modeling their ability to catch dinner? Do they believe this display of dominance over a literal salmon will spark some deep hunger in the womb of someone of childbearing age?

All I am certain of is that it does not work. Modern users of the Tinder app consider a shit-eating grin on the face of a man hoisting a carcass in the air a great red flag. Even the girls who hunt and fish have adapted to understand that the dead-fish pic is a key indicator of a Fuckboy on the prowl.

My functioning theory for the overpopulation of fish pics is simply a lack of options. Men rarely take photos of themselves and their friends in their daily lives, and only *do* take photos doing activities deemed masculine enough to capture. Preserving memories of authentic and spontaneous moments is often a task relegated to mothers, sisters, and wives. Taking photos of *oneself* in the form of what is colloquially called a "selfie" is considered a great vanity. As such, a photo of oneself that is not in fish format may be something that men with brains poisoned by the toxic dribble of misogyny believe is beneath them—or particularly *feminine.*

That men may not have many photos of themselves brings me a great sadness, for I wonder how many vibrant, beautiful lives have passed by unobserved and unacknowledged.

Recommendation: Men of all ages should freshly decide that *not having memories of their life* does not make them more of a man. They *can* and *should* stop to take photos of themselves as they are living. They might use the self-timer, ask a kind stranger to take their photo, or indulge in a cheeky selfie. They will thank themselves someday for the road map back to lost places they once loved. Life, no matter how brilliant, has a way of fading in our minds unless we mark a trail back to those bright spots. They will then be capable of creating a bangin' Tinder profile with photos showcasing a well-rounded, fun, friendly person who has many hobbies beyond luring an unsuspecting creature into their grasp and clubbing it on the head.

2. The Jokes about Impaired Judgment Philosophy

Usually seen as a statement in the biography like, "I'm a 4, but I'll buy you drinks until I look like a 10!" Variations of this joke are, unfortunately, quite common in the profiles of men, and it perplexes me that this must be explained. I can only conclude two things:

1. Men do not have a consistent sense of responsibility toward policing the shit out of each other when making rape jokes, so they go unquestioned.

2. *Not* experiencing the threat and fear of knowing that many people want to incapacitate and harm you at all times[4] has led the menfolk to miss the crucial failing in this strategy: promising to ply a woman with enough alcohol to impair her judgment and alter her perception of a man is not a joke, it is a threat.

Recommendation: Take this joke off your profiles, ye who do not wish to be rapey.

3. The Girls Take Themselves Too Seriously and Don't Understand Dark Humor Philosophy[5]

"Looking for a girl who doesn't take herself too seriously" has become increasingly common on the profiles I have observed in the Tinderlands. It is more insidious than it presents.

Indeed, "You shouldn't take yourself too seriously" appears innocuous enough. However, its appearance en masse as a uniting cry for single men left me wondering, *Why?* It certainly implies that there is a drought of female partners who have a carefree and fun attitude. When considered in conjunction with the equally troublesome "Looking for a girl who

4. What must that be like? To order a drink and not wonder if it's drugged?
5. See also: "I have a dark sense of humor, so I hope you can take a joke" and "fluent in sarcasm, need a girl who can keep up!"

can take a joke," a pattern is revealed. It appears the belief that women are too sensitive and too passionate about, presumably, issues that greatly affect them and those they love is a culturally held belief amongst some single men.

Thus the phrase betrays the hidden truths of the Fuckboy brain. Fuckboys do not consider the issues that affect others "their problem." Fuckboys dismiss valid anger, rage, annoyance, and fear in response to threatening beliefs as oversensitivity. Fuckboys believe that there is nothing wrong with how they see the world and that fussy women are simply overreacting, so they declare they are on the hunt for the "chill girl" who knows a racist joke or a rape joke is just the quirky offspring of a bold man and his "dark" sense of humor.

Recommendation: Taking women a bit more seriously and practicing self-reflection instead of deflection would get the menfolk off Tinder much more quickly than suggesting that women are all a little uptight and a little bit of a joke.

4. The "My Soulmate Will Love Star Wars/Marvel/ Gaming/the Gym" Philosophy[6]

There is an unnerving consistency to the hobbies that the menfolk list. Approximately eighty-five percent of the male Tinder demographic I observed are only passionate about the same four things: Star Wars, Marvel, gaming, and the gym.

---

6. Usually followed by: "Would be nice to find a girl who actually shares my interests."

I do not claim that those hobbies and interests are not *good* or that they are something to be ashamed of. However, they are not commonly shared by the female population.

Star Wars and Marvel were not made for women to feel connected to or represented by, and spaces celebrating the two franchises are traditionally very hostile to anyone who might qualify as "diverse."[7]

The gaming community was gatekept by the male population from its creation. Even now, female streamers and gamers experience brutal harassment at an alarming rate at the hands of men who feel threatened by their presence in the traditionally masculine space. In some cases "being into gaming" has been a measuring stick used by men to provide or deny access into the coveted club of being a "cool girl," therefore enforcing the "she's not like other girls" trope[8] and forcing girls to conform to the spaces and interests of men to be afforded kind treatment.

The gym is not a welcoming space for most women. There are, of course, women who love the gym and who are deeply passionate about fitness as a science and practice. However, even the women with the bodies most celebrated by society cannot go to a gym without being the subject of unwanted attention. The gym is a place where women are ogled. It is a place where men feel a sense of ownership, and so they are

---

7. Star Wars Bros and Marvel Bros are notoriously some of the most toxic incel douchebags on the internet. They have literally started campaigns to bomb the release of Marvel movies starring diverse casts simply because they don't want to let anyone else look like a superhero.

8. Being told you're "not like other girls" as a compliment is to be told "I'm a misogynist, but you're palatable!"

often compelled to protect that feeling of power by asserting their dominance over the women they are "tolerating" in their space. There are endless records on the internet of men cutting into a woman's workout to mansplain equipment to her (often incorrectly).

Women who do *not* have the type of body that is deemed gymworthy often find the gym a place of great threat and hostility. To be a fat woman in a gym is to be constantly harassed, judged, and turned into an object of disgust and fascination by the men inside. It is not a place of fun or peace.

The expectation that women should be invested in these hobbies at the same rate as men is, at minimum, misguided.

Perhaps there is a lack of diversity in the hobbies of men because they are not afforded the freedom to explore more things. Much of what makes life beautiful, from art to music to dance to food and drink, is often miscategorized as inherently feminine unless placed in the realm of highly competitive professionals.[9] In their endless encouragement to establish a rock-hard masculinity, I wonder if boys are not given the opportunity to explore what their souls are curious about. I wonder if they are steered down rigid pathways toward war, stories of heroes wearing the American flag, first-person shooter games, and building larger bodies capable of subduing smaller ones. I wonder if they were ever given nail polish to see what their bodies look like in color, or given

9. Cooking is for women, unless you're a head chef. Dancing is for women, unless you're in the Jabbawockeez. Art is for women, unless you're Banksy or Michelangelo.

a watercolor set and told to paint what they can see from their backyard. I imagine many little boys spent days in the woods with the men, learning how to hunt something and consume it, while their sisters stayed in the kitchen with the women, learning how to create nourishment from scratch.

Recommendation: Menfolk who do not wish to be swept left upon immediately should consider their hobbies with intention. If those are the only things they love, that is completely fine, but they should ask themselves if their hobbies are entirely *theirs*, or if, perhaps, they were assigned to them as a way to further define their masculinity. There is no such thing as something one loves making him more or less of a man. Further, the expectation that a female partner should love all of the same things is unreasonable. They must expand their minds and think of other things they might be interested in that stand on more neutral ground. Perhaps start with things they have always been curious about but have not explored. The people they are chatting with, in hopes that they find someone who makes their heart skip a beat, may have something they love that *they* could share. There are no doubt many ways to experience the world they have not yet tried. There is still curiosity in us all.

5. The "Any Chick on Here Not Crazy?" Philosophy

Recommendation: Fuck off.

6. The "She Wants a Piece of My Man Meat" Philosophy

There appears to be a disconnect between the photos men *believe* will secure them a female mate and the photos that

actually inspire interest in potential partners. I have dis-
cussed the Bitches Love Fishes photo, but I have yet to
expand on the other photos that may appear in the carou-
sel of a wild Fuckboy.

As I have waded my way through the toxic sludge of this
place in pursuit of the ever-illusive clarity all singles crave,
I have observed a consistency in Fuckboy photo strategy.
They will employ any combination of the following:

- **Expensive car:** they may or may not be staged on or in
  said vehicle—and there is a *very* good chance they do
  not own this vehicle at all.
- **Gym pic:** with biceps / with hiked-up shorts to show
  thighs / with shirt pulled up to show abs / entirely
  shirtless.
- **Bathroom mirror pic:** usually used to betray the existence of a large penis, either in some form of threadbare
  undergarment or athletic trousers pulled low on hip
  bones to communicate that they can, in fact, come all
  the way off.
- **Drunk as fuck with the lads pic.**
- **Creepy expressionless selfie pic.**
- **Random animal photo they are not even in.**

When observed as a whole, the photos routinely chosen by
the Fuckboy serve to communicate some core messaging.
The expensive vehicle indicates that the Fuckboy is wealthy.
The various gym photos indicate the Fuckboy has a body
deemed as worthy and fuckable, as well as raw physical
strength. The penis pics are almost exclusively of large penises, and as such, they communicate that they have what

they believe is sexual prowess and power. The drunk photos with friends attempt to show a fun mate who is desirable to be around and accepted into groups of traditionally masculine people. The creepy selfie shows the required face but does not betray the softness of emotion. The random animal is a transparent attempt to give what they believe females desire—to lure women to have sex with them in response to being gifted with doggies and kitties.

These photos are intended to appeal to the gaze of women, but in reality, appeal more broadly and successfully to that of other men. We are usually unconscious of the way sexual preferences are dictated to us by the people deciding what stories to tell and what images to label as "desirable." Any woman knows the pervasiveness of "sexy" as defined by the media, and its control over groupthink.

Fuckboys, in particular, seek out a female partner who is slim and fit, with a body that meets the standards of fuckability as established by men in power. They seek out a partner who exhibits only traits of traditional femininity—often claiming to look for "bubbly, outgoing, fun-loving, caring women who don't take themselves too seriously."

In turn, they expect a *woman* desires a man who exhibits only traditional masculinity, so they post photos of themselves as providers; as stern and emotionless; as physically strong, dominating, and hard; as sexually desirable; and as an accepted member of a pack of ultramasculine men participating in ultramasculine behavior. The animal photos are just a bit of blatant grafting.

The sort of females searching for meaningful connections in the desert of Tinder are, of course, diverse. Some are seeking out casual sexual encounters. Some want fun flings. Others are seeking a more consistent relationship. None, in my observation, are seeking out something boring and vaguely threatening, like a car and a dick and a photo of arms that might try to choke them against their will.[10]

Recommendation: Menfolk attempting to communicate a more meaningful self and curate a profile catered to the interests of women should share honest photos of their life. Examples include photos of themselves doing something they are passionate about beyond choking down preworkout on leg day, photos of themselves happy with the people they genuinely love, in which they are being gentle and tender. Photos of being caring, cooking, or taking care of something special.

———

I hope these notes have shed some light on the question that plagues all singles: How the fuck am I supposed to meet someone on dating apps, and how the fuck am I supposed to *not?* It has been many moons since one could hope to fall in love over a shared milkshake at a soda parlor, and dating apps seem to be the only reliable modern option. Perhaps there is a way to make dating more doable. Perhaps with a more thoughtful representation of self, rather than a copy and paste of the repulsive Fuckboy strategy, there will be a better chance for like-minded people to fall in love.

10. May we take a moment to say, if you are a man who wants to participate in power dynamic play, learn how to do so ethically and safely before you ever put your hand on a woman's throat. Duh.

Summary

It is my strong conclusion that placing the burden of self-actualization and self-reflection on a single person in a proposed partnership to secure a strong and steady match is not working. Furthermore, the ways the potential partners of cis-straight men are told to change are often tactics to uphold the oppressive social structure of the patriarchy, and do not yield authentic affection or love, but maintain unequal power. As such, I implore those who wish to be partnered with cis-straight men to see themselves as already whole and to encourage their potential mates to be the ones who dig deep.

My professional recommendation is for everyone to bring their most authentic, most vulnerable self if they are looking for someone who *actually likes them*. First, go in search of who you really might be without the influence of who you *thought you should* be, or who you were told to be in order to conform to gender stereotypes, or who you *thought* a potential partner would want to be with. The basics of what we find attractive are pretty simple when you think about it. Radical authenticity requires courage. So does falling in love.

Signed from the listless lands of Tinder,

Another Amateur Anthropologist Searching for Truth

Brother

I cannot help but hate you
for what you have not gone through—
for the danger and pain no one expects you to endure.

I have to work much harder
to stay open and good-hearted
while I am condemned, followed home, and hurt.

Then again, I wonder,
does kindness still come easy
to a man who can walk where he chooses to go?

From whom is gentleness farther—
the hunter or the deer—
when He only hears yes, and She only hears no?

portrait of a good man

I don't hate men.[1]

(Men, I need you to stick with me on this one.)

I am sure, especially in the wake of this book, I will be *accused* of hating men—but the simple fact is, I do not. I quite like men. I like to date men. There are many men in my life whom I dearly and desperately love.[2]

When we speak in generalities about men, we speak to the entire group, and to what the group is responsible for. As is true in any discussion of a group versus an individual, not everything said applies to every person in the group. Anyone with compassion and empathy should be able to hear a statement about a group they are a part of that doesn't necessarily apply to *them*, but that *does* apply statistically to the entire monolith, and understand that *it is not personal*, and it can still be true.

1. For the sake of this essay, I am going to be using the term "men" to refer to cis, straight, (mostly) white men. Other men are of course fucking valid. But I don't want to type—nor do you want to read—cis straight white men seven hundred times.

2. This particular entry is dedicated to my siblings and my dad, whom I dearly and desperately love.

So when I talk about the suffering that men have caused, I mean that men are responsible for the fact that every year I was in college at least one of my roommates was raped, and for the fact that I have been followed in the dark too many times to count, and for the fact that I am afraid of going to a grocery store in America where there might be a man with a gun.[3] I mean that women and LGBTQ+ people cannot go a day without fearing being subjected to the violence many men resort to when they feel powerless. I mean that we cannot afford to give men the benefit of the doubt and hope that they are *good*, because the stakes for us are survival.

Good men can listen to us, hear what we have endured under the system they thrive in, and know that it is true. They can listen without being defensive or excusing themselves from the problem. They can be curious and feel a righteous calling to use their power to change things.

But I know it must also be very painful to suddenly be the bad guy in every story. It cannot feel great to look in the mirror and see so many similarities to the people being exposed as the evil final boss fight, especially after so many years of being held up as the good guy. After growing up watching superhero movies and war dramas and stories of guys who look like you swooping in to save the girl and the country and goodness itself, suddenly being the villain people don't trust must be really disorienting. I know it must feel hurtful to be assumed to be harmful before you're even known. It must take a lot of courage and self-compassion to keep feeling good about yourself when so many people who share your identity are responsible for causing so much pain.

3. I have personalized experiences that you can generalize to every woman in America. We all have a friend who has been raped, if it isn't us. We have all been followed. We have all known the fear of gun violence and male rage.

That sucks.

I'm not invalidating any of that, but it must be said that so many of the feelings white people, and especially white men, are experiencing right now are (1) feelings we bought and paid for with really awful behavior over time and place (we don't get to separate ourselves from our history and the privileges we inherited, nor the fallout), and (2) feelings that have been inflicted upon oppressed groups who did *not* buy and pay for that treatment. How many different races and sexualities and genders and religions have been villainized by white America? By cis men? It sucks to feel that way, but it also just might be our turn. And when we find ourselves suffering under the pressure of the systems we built, there is no one to blame but us.

I have sat with some of the aforementioned men who I love so very dearly and heard them express their pain and confusion. They are very good people, with very good hearts, who sit and listen and don't fight back when people talk about the hurt they have collectively caused. They are the sort of men who say "that's because men are garbage" when you say that one in six women have been raped. They are the sort of men who are content with being quiet in rooms where their peers would talk over everyone else. They are good people, and they are hurting under the weight of group accountability.

The hard part about that pain is that only they can make it leave. I wish that I could touch their chest and pull it out of their hearts. I'd stuff it into the barrel of a gun and fire it into a man who deserved it—of one who felt no shame at all. But I can't.

The only way for good men to absolve themselves of the hurt they feel while they reckon with their legacy is for men to hold other men accountable. In droves. In masses. In giant, mutinous ways. It is for men to forsake entirely their unjustly held power and betray the cult of Patriarchy. Men have to overthrow their own. They have to insist on power being shifted away from majority male holdings. They have to insist men are held to the highest standard of justice for things they have gotten away with for centuries. They must truly and terribly turn their backs on the very club that has put them in positions of access to safety, success, and power. They must relinquish those things to stop the churning of the machine, because only *they* can. Until then, the machine will continue to use the rest of us like fuel—breaking us up and burning us down—and we will continue to do what we must to keep ourselves safe. We will continue to move through the world as though men are guilty until they can prove they are not.

That doesn't really happen overnight.

It's possible that the good men walking amongst us now will spend their lifetime carrying an unequal burden of guilt and shame, while their peers continue to harm with abandon. It's possible that their sons will carry the burden too. They might be the guy who looks like everyone's least favorite person in every room for the rest of their lives.

That sounds really terrible. And honestly, really unfair.

Even men suffer at the hands of men.[4]

But I am thankful for you—for the ones who do their best to stop the cycles of pain and danger. It is not in vain.

One of the most honest expressions of love and gratitude a person can create for another is to capture them in art. To find them so inspiring and wonderful, they have to press them down in paint, sew them into fabric, harvest them in words—just so they can always remember what they were like in that *one* moment. Just so they can have them to love forever. And

---

4. This is true in a lot of ways. There are very few in the large number of men who a Patriarchy helps but does not harm at all.

just to make sure the one they love can see themselves in the same glorious light that they do.

I don't have a lot, but I have a few pages and a little bit of time. The following is a portrait of the good men in my life drawn from who I have known them to be.[5]

You are a gentle man. I have heard your voice drop the hard edges as you use everything you can to make a small being feel safe in a world so very big. I have watched you cup a butterfly with a broken wing and search the garden for the most peaceful place, then nestle its fragile body there. You bend down to the ground, no matter all the creaking of your long-day bones, to meet a child at eye level, to make them feel important. You reach out so tenderly to a heart that is sore.

You are a caring man. I have felt your hand upon my back as I wept into the bed. I have known the comfort of your silence as you stayed with me, even as the sun abandoned the sky, to prove to me I was not alone. I have awoken to find the very thing I mentioned I wanted but could not afford waiting on my doorstep. Your name appears on the screen of my phone when the days are too hard. You remember the details of a life that is not yours, asking in earnest about things mentioned in passing a month or a year ago.

You are a generous man. You drive for days to help a friend in need. You open your wallet when there is not much to spare, only to make sure your people don't have to share the strain. You give away the things that you have loved because someone else might need them more just then. Then you give away your time because someone else might need it more just then. You absorb

---

5. The good men everywhere.

the blows meant for others. You stay quiet to soothe the anger when you have every right to speak. You have picked me up from airports, and driven me home after too many margaritas, then driven me back in the morning to retrieve my abandoned car. You have come to all the faraway places I insist on making home, just so I do not feel on my own.

You are a thoughtful man. Your face lights up while you explain your mother's Christmas gift, and how hard you looked to find the perfect thing. You seek to include when it does not cross others' minds. I have talked to you while you shopped for a very complicated dinner because you thought a four-hour simmer was a small sacrifice to comfort the one you love after a very weary day.

You are a nurturing man. You forsake your plans when there is a lost-looking pet on the side of the road. You never question if the cost was worth the care for the lives you feel responsible for. You set the table, make the dinner, pour the wine, and do the dishes before bed, so no one wakes up to them in the morning. You squint and focus as you trim the leaves on a tiny plant. You smile at the cat sleeping on your freshly washed laundry. You meet the pain in another and offer to take it on instead for a little while.

You are a creative man. Your mind spins worlds out of nothing, plucks stories from the air. You paint into being something only you could see before. You take something that isn't quite fitting and change it until it feels like it's always been yours.

You are a curious man. You try new things that you will very likely fail at, just because you haven't tried them before. You ask in earnest after someone else's interests because they know so much that you do not. You travel somewhere new, again and again, intent on finding everything life has to offer you. You shed your skin and become someone new again, and again, as you learn more about who you want to be.

You are a courageous man. You stand up to people who could hurt you, so someone else will not have to. You turn your back on the rules prescribed to you and are true to who you are. You reject the toxicity of your fathers. You defy the expectation of your friends. You paint your nails, and learn to dance, and fall wildly, recklessly in love. I have listened to your anger at the way your sister has inherited a different world than your brother. I have always counted on you as a safe place to bring my own rage, to trade it in for validation and the room to breathe. You boldly stare down the uncertainty of life, committed to being steady for the people who rely on your strength. You cry under a starlit night so perfect that it breaks your gentle heart.

You are a good man. You teach your sons how to help and how to heal. You do not force yourself upon others. You do not take what is not yours. You do not hoard what you have. You are kind, and you are smart, and you are compassionate. You listen and learn. You apologize and you change. You feel deeply and without shame, for you know to feel is to be alive. You are a safe place in a violent storm. You are the feeling of home. You are the warmth on a long, cold night. You are the laughter in a season of endless, ceaseless grief.

To the good men—I do not hate you. Not at all.

I need you. I love you. Dearly and desperately.

Please, *stay good.*

am i still a good person if i keep waxing my pubes?

Here's the thing.

I really want to be the sort of feminist who doesn't shave and doesn't wear bras and who's never even *contemplated* Botox. I *want* to not give a hoot if I terrify children with the ominous *clap-clap-clap* of my sweat-sock knockers slapping against my belly as I descend a flight of stairs.

I'm not though. I wear bras, goddamnit. (*For the children.*)

I shave my legs *and* armpits. I invest in anti-wrinkle lotions and potions at a financially irresponsible level. For a long time, I felt pretty good about these small battles lost in the larger war for liberation, even though I know they are all dictated by the impossible ways women are meant to stay young and hairless forever. Despite my lotions and underwire, I still felt like I was winning overall because I had one critical battlefield of my body that I had never yielded to the enemy. I, unlike almost every one of my contemporaries, absolutely refused to shave my pubes.

I was cruising through life with a pristine, natural forest. I wasn't having sex, so there were no invasive species to disrupt the indigenous landscape. I was rarely swimming, and when I did it was rarely with anyone I had motive to impress. For the most part, I was just vibing au naturel and feeling marginally superior to the gals who were going full baby seal.[1]

Then I got horny. I got horny for men.

It is incredible how quickly this can ruin so much.

So I started cruising the dating apps. I became obsessed with the notion of finding a man who I didn't think would murder me to plant his flag in my undiscovered territory. And suddenly, for no reason at all, I decided that I absolutely *had* to shave my pubes with whatever tools were handy.

Guess what? That was a very bad choice.

I didn't even get the last straggler out of my razor blades before I was possessed with an unholy itching. *Oh my absolute god.* You know what you're not really allowed to do in polite company? Scratch your crotch like a monkey. Grocery stores don't love seeing your mitts on your bits before you start opening egg cartons to inspect the goods. So I suffered, and I languished, and I mourned the days before I decided to take a hacksaw to my gated garden. Everything was inflamed, everything was painful, and absolutely everything was itchy. What was I thinking?

I reached out to friends for emotional support and for confirmation that I was not the only person on Earth being punished with a witch's curse for bowing to beauty standards. They informed me that shaving was a dingbat fucking idea, but waxing is where the money is.

I didn't care about what "worked," I was never doing that again. Turns out the most effective way to smother the fire of lust is to start the fire of a poorly shaven hoo-ha. So I went through

---

1. A key part of nullifying the cognitive dissonance of your *own* behaviors, like shaving your legs and getting Botox even though you're vehemently opposed to the male gaze, is to find ways that you're not as bad as other people. Duh.

a painstaking regrowth period, during which I absolutely DID NOT want a man getting anywhere near my mangled parts, and I was back to normal.

I had learned my lesson. I had sacrificed my last bastion of resistance to the pervasive cause of patriarchy, and I had suffered a swift and bumpy retribution. I was no longer a weak-willed daughter of the rebellion, but the Joan of Arc of pubic liberty! I was furry and free! I was a true hero in the timeless fight for women's equality and the freedom to do what we want with our bodies! I was liking every meme I saw on Instagram about men just *dealing* with pubic hair, because nature is beautiful, ya caveman nasties! I was brave! I was immovable! I was . . .

. . . horny again.

Did you know the European Wax Center gives you your first wax for free?

I booked a Brazilian, because, like most things in my life, I didn't believe in the walk-slowly-into-the-shallow-end approach. I'm more of an all-or-nothing kind of guy, prone to ripping off the Band-Aid, or in this case, the butt strip.

I had been promised by friends that waxing would result in far less misery. It was quick, only a little painful, then you're free as an eel to slip and slide your way into hedonic bliss. And let me tell ya, when I left that table and strutted my stuff to my car, I was *living*. Wow, what a sensation. What an honest to god experience. I'm not gonna lie—being smooth as a cue ball down there is nice as cuss. I understood why we were all getting waxed now. It wasn't for the sake of frictionless sex with men, it was for the sheer pleasure of having a silky little secret. So clean. So fresh. So effortlessly luxurious.

Then, hair does what hair do, and those curlies regrew. They brought with them an onslaught of ingrowns the likes of which I had never experienced before. It wasn't just war, it was a textbook massacre, and every pore was the site of another slaughter. Why my body decided to permanently seal every follicle immediately upon its residents taking a brief vacation, I will never know. I only know that my wax had conjured the haunted Triangle of Death out of what was once the Pleasure Pillow.

When I found myself two months later still trying to salvage the remains of a once lush rainforest, I thought, *Nope. This is really not worth it.*

But my toxic trait is that I refuse to learn if I don't wanna.

The next time I went through with a wax, I had a man lined up for a romp a few days post-hot-yoink. It was the perfect window between the initial irritation and the prolonged suffering that paced in the shadows. And honestly? It was great. I felt hot and sexy and very touchable. I wasn't self-conscious about what he thought about pubic hair, and the night was super fun. The man was delicious. I was like, *yes, so glad we did this*.[2]

Flash forward four months. It was 3:00 a.m., and I was alone in my apartment maniacally trying to finish a manuscript. I hadn't seen the sun in three days and had woken up from a fitful nap with a Dorito stuck to my arm without any recollection of eating Doritos. But despite my looming deadlines and deteriorating stability, my laptop lay abandoned on the couch. Netflix played to an empty room. A cursor blinked into the dark on a blank page. Because I wasn't there.

I was in the bathroom, folded in half like a determined croissant, digging into my tender flesh with tweezers so sharp I am always shocked when they let me bring them onto airplanes. A gremlin in the harsh light of a midnight bathroom, not doing

---

2. "This" being getting the hairs ripped out of my body so I didn't have to navigate the minefield of men's hot takes on women's body hair before I got laid.

my job and not being asleep, going full Indiana Jones and the Temple of Ingrowns.

The knowledge that I had rogue hairs trapped beneath my skin at all times—causing chaos, and scarring, and unsightly, unpleasant topography where there was once the kind of natural beauty John Denver might sing about—was too much for me to bear. As my faculties waned under the pressure of deadlines, isolation, and sleep deprivation, the thought had begun kicking down the door of my brain, clanging pots and pans, and sneering at me:

"A single pubic hair has bested you for four months. How can you finish a book if you can't even grow pubes without incident? Fifteen-year-old dingbats can grow pubes, and they can't even drive, you guppy. They can't even see a scary movie without their mommy. Do you need your mommy? You are an impostor. Here, have a syndrome about it. Neener fuckin' neener."

Neener-neener my butt!!! My desire to evict subterranean Goldilocks from my Mama Bear bed occluded every rational thought. I had tried and failed to find the beast deep in its lair a million times before. I had drawn blood, over and over. I had risked infection.[3] I had (probably) narrowly escaped death. Now intrusive thoughts about my incompetence were calling to me during the witching hour, and enough was enough.

Fueled by feral rage and the iron will of a hero at the climax of their journey, I hooked that little bitch like a born angler. There on the toilet, cackling like the Joker with a single twitching eye, I held my prize to the light. By god, she was a terrible beauty. Rapunzel could have tossed that thing over her shoulder

---

3. Listen, if you think this is the description of someone who takes the time to disinfect their pointy bois between every spelunking mission, you are the sort of optimist that I can't be around. Good for you.

and been on her way to a brand-new life. I felt the way men must feel when they stand next to a seven-foot marlin they snagged off the coast of wherever-the-fuck. The relief that washed over me as I gazed upon my long-sought prize was like nothing I'd ever experienced. I was invincible. I was floating. I could fight God.

Now, if you were to look at my gossipy text messages in the wake of the hot-hairless hookup compared to the ones I sent moments after I vanquished my subdermal foe, you'd find that I texted more people, more excitedly, and with more juicy detail, about my ingrown hair. Sex was hot, but beating the pube was divine. The moment I first realized I *had it* in my pointy grasp played in my mind on a delicious loop. Sex didn't make me feel like I'd won a Herculean struggle. There is nothing quite like realizing that you have finally restored something wrong to being right.

What's the verdict, then? Am I a gender traitor for enjoying the feeling of being waxed though I know I'll pay for it? For feeling some sort of raw power when I'm freshly smooth, even if it is likely directed by scripts of patriarchal sexuality? Am I a good feminist for growing out my body hair . . . until there's a man in the house? Technically, I don't do it to please the men, I do it to reduce the friction between me and having a nice time in my body. I do it for my own comfort. And sure, I probably wouldn't feel compelled to go hairless if it weren't very well known that it is the preferred style of grooming for most cis men, but am I betraying the cause by doing what makes me feel good in my own skin? It's not my fault the world is wired this way. I can't single-handedly undo it all by being like, "*Welcome to the jungle, Tarzan,*" so is it still my job?

I love the feeling of a fresh wax. I love the feeling of eliminating roadblocks between my body and being seen as conventionally attractive. Life is easier for people cis men think are sexy than it is for people they don't. Is it a sin to choose ease?

And yet, I hate the cost I pay. I hate the feeling of my body being knotted up in the wake of a sacrifice. I hate the ping of shame I feel when my hair and money get tossed away and I can practically hear the great feminist icons of the past issue a collective sigh.

Perhaps there is no answer. Perhaps there is no verdict. Perhaps we all make the best choices we can when every action has its cost. We cannot change everything at once, and yet we must keep choosing amidst the system set up to fail us. How can we blame someone else for the things we choose? Then again, how can we not? The only conclusion I can comfortably draw is this: we do the best we can, and we need grace while we do it. Sometimes the righteous fist of justice brings more damage than relief. Sometimes we need the gentle hands of compassion.

No one is a perfect example of a feminist, or of a good man, or of a good mother. No one is a perfect ally, or perfect reformer, or a perfect liberationist. Everyone gets tired. Everyone has to sometimes choose between one hard thing and another. We are only human, after all.

And while I hope that the people I love always encourage my progress toward the path of an equal and kind world, I also hope that we can be nuanced enough to offer a soft place to land when the choices we have leave us feeling a little heartsore and unsteady. I refuse to live my life *clap-clapping* around town drenched in unrighteous boob sweat. I'm getting an underwire bra, and I don't want to hear a single snide word about the male gaze.

A wise man once told me, "There is so much gray to sift through, and there are no easy answers. I do the best I can with the information I have, I honor the limits of my mind and body, and I choose with the intention of doing the most good for the most people. I am content knowing that should I face a higher power, and should they ask, 'What do you have to say for yourself?' I could honestly say that if I was wrong, I was wrong for the right reasons. That's enough for me."

I have used that lesson as a lens against my life many times, and it has soothed the turmoil of a conflicted heart more than once.

If I am wrong, am I wrong for the right reasons?

If my answer is yes, me and my well-supported tataroonies can live with that.

Poems about Self-Love

I'm sick of simple poems about self-love—
as if a mantra in the mirror can drown the pounding door?

What a shallow way to cure the cinder block chest
that costs us everything, *everything,*
to breathe through.

Every woman I know is tired just from being here.

the righteous anger
of the swindled
& starving

Ready for a deeply original thought?

I wish I knew then what I know now.

I doubt there's a person on Earth who doesn't have something they'd kill to transmute through time and space into the head of their oblivious teenage self to change the course of their life.

If we could mail a letter back in time to our younger selves, some of us might try to stop the cutting of bangs with kitchen scissors. Maybe we'd beg ourselves not to date that one guy, or cheat on that one test, or go for the feather tattoo behind our ear.[1] Some of us might try to save our eyebrows from the fateful trend of the 2000s. I suffered from overplucking the center bit—terrified of inheriting my father's unruly unibrow for which he is famous in the family's oral history. I only avoided the fate of the Pencil-Browed-2000s-It-Girl because my mom looked at me from across the kitchen one day and announced, "Devrie,

---

1. If you love your feather ear tattoo, you *love your feather ear tattoo* and what the hell do I know?

your eyebrows look like two caterpillars racing to see which can crawl off the side of your face faster."

If *I* could meet my fourteen-year-old self—that little teacher's pet in her plastic headband and sideswept bangs—I'd hit her with a speech so passionate it would make Shakespeare drop hot, fat tears onto his pantaloons. I'm talking about a Shonda Rhimes–style monologue.[2] I love *Grey's Anatomy*, so a Shondalogue would have the best chance of cutting through the hubris of youth and finding its way into my underdeveloped brain. I'd trap my younger self in, like, an elevator or a stairwell to deliver the heartfelt plea. I would look into her eyes, hold her acne-face in my hands, and beg her to hear the one thing I wish she'd known more than anything else:

Life is not on the other side of a different body, and you don't need to change before you can experience a brilliant life or a brilliant love.

Even if I could manage to crack the mystery of time travel and *not* collapse the universe by talking to younger me, that stubborn girl wouldn't believe me anyway. To be a young woman with a body that was built to carry weight, starch, and children during the Obesity Epidemic era was to know that you were responsible for the weakening of America by being a size 10. *America's Next Top Model, The Swan, Biggest Loser*—all television you tuned into with your family. And if you were properly plus size? Fuck you, for real. Paris Hilton and Blake Lively were the ultimate body goals then, and their jeans were held aloft only by pubic bones that appeared to be on the verge of a nervous breakdown. It was not a good time to be built like an average teenager with pubic bones that seemed very well adjusted, much less a plus-sized teenager. I believed I needed to change with every fiber of my being.

2. "Pick *me*, choose *me*, love *me*."

Then again, who am I to say time travel isn't real? So just in case she *is* listening, little me somewhere, cursing the low-rise jean and wondering if the kid with the perfectly flippy blond hair likes her back,[3] I'll say it anyway:

Babe, *this is it*. This is your one life. We get one shot, and no one knows what happens next, so the way we spend our time matters. It matters a lot, and there isn't much time to spare. Now brace yourself, because here comes the hard part that I only know because I've already been there. You know that milestone you're waiting for before you're gonna allow yourself to be happy? You never reach it.

You never reach the goal weight, or the goal appearance, because the goalpost moves. It's cruel, and it's unfair, and it's not always *you* who's moving it, because *you're not supposed to be happy with your body*. There are a lot of forces spending a lot of money to make sure you're *never* happy with your body. They want you to be in a constant state of wanting—for you to be searching for a solution to your wrongness, your unlovable softness, your *too flat, too low, too thin, too big, too old*. There is a full boardroom somewhere where they're drinking expensive whisky and toasting to the fact that you think you're not worthy of happiness because your body is unacceptable. Your misery is their yacht money, and they will *never* invite you on the yacht. *Bastards*.

So hear me when I tell you again: *you'll never reach it. You have to let it go.*

And I know that hurts to hear since we try so hard, and sometimes we try so long. Even worse—a lot of us sacrifice to get there. We sacrifice, believing that when we finally make it, all of the precious things we gave up on the way will be worth the destination of happiness, but we never arrive.

---

3. Spoiler alert: *he didn't.*

I'm so sorry that there is so much to grieve.[4]

But the bottom line is—*it's a lie*. There is no version of you on the other side of the size 6 door you are trying so hard to fit through. There is no you waiting to be unearthed so you can finally start living the life you deserve. It's just *this* you, and it's only *this* now, and time is ticking by.

You can't put off living your only life in the hope that you'll discover the secret to becoming good enough. If you put your life off until all of that comes true, you'll be putting your life off until you're dead.

Did you know that the overwhelming majority of diets don't work?[5] Not only do they not work, they mostly backfire. They are costly in both money and health, weakening the body and sucking up all our spare resources. Typically, people gain back more weight than they lost, because bodies don't like to change. They want to keep us stable and protect us. Bodies are like the people who love us, that way.

If there was really a perfect nose, or perfect hair, or a perfect shape, wouldn't there be more people who look that way? Perfection would be stable, and our goalposts would be the same ones our grandmothers strove toward. But the beauty standard is completely redefined every five years or so because once enough people have spent enough to look "perfect," they don't need to spend money anymore.

This is how they rob us—by refusing to acknowledge the truth. The truth is costly. If you know how routinely diets fail, you don't care so much about spending on the new weight-loss

---

4. Many of us have given up a lot in pursuit of thinness or a perfect body. It demands a certain grief for the lost time and the lost chances. You're allowed to feel that.

5. This is a widely understood fact with data to back it up—you may Google it.

program or the new diet pill or the new body trainer. If you're already as beautiful as you can be, you don't need to spend money in pursuit of perfection. That costs the shareholders and stakeholders and capitalism beneficiaries to lose out on profits. The *truth* means that Richard gets one less yacht, and Baby Dickie *loves* his yachts! Baby Dickie[6] want big boatie, goddamnit!

So, if for no other reason than the righteous indignance of the swindled and scammed, ditch the dieting thing. Ditch the self-loathing and self-hatred and deprivation. Ditch the upholding of a system that forces other women to adhere to the terms and conditions of "acceptable womanhood."[7] Don't make it about self-love, make it about justice. I am much more motivated by taking down a selfish a-hole who's hurting others than by self-loving and being warm and fuzzy. Why should Baby Dickie get to turn your life into a miserable collage of carrot sticks tip-dipped in fat-free ranch and surgery scars, so that *he* can die of a heart attack at eighty-five, sandwiched between two twentysomethings on a boat off the coast of Greece? Dead and rich off the profits of your life unlived?

Now, I know that you might be thinking, "It's not that easy!"

I get it, I really do. We are wired to model behavior. The stories we're told don't usually have people that look like us doing the things we dream of doing. We understand the world based on what we have been told about it, shown about it. Going out on a limb and trying something you haven't seen someone pull off before is daunting. It takes gumption to start living a life

---

6. Apologies to my grandfather (who art in heaven) who was named Richard and went by Grandpa Dick. I have never thought of you as a Baby Dickie. This I swear. Please don't haunt me.

7. There is a lot of compelling research linking our obsession with thinness directly to whiteness and a desire to distance ourselves from the Black body. Check out *Fearing the Black Body: The Racial Origins of Fatphobia* by Sabrina Strings for a start!

you have never been given a road map for. It takes courage to bet on yourself when you've never seen it done.

But, babe, you can prove them all wrong. It might be lonely to be the person going first, but it's so much better than being stuck in a crowd of people who are afraid and who don't believe you deserve a big, beautiful life.

What have you been holding back from while you waited to become worthy? Quit the job that makes you small, and get on the road toward the place that you've always felt called to or where you first felt the feeling of home. Maybe you've never seen a Nancy Meyers leading lady who looks like you do, but that's hardly enough reason to resign to a small life, right?

Right?

You are worthy of love *right now*.

You *deserve* love right now.

You deserve a kiss that feels like the sky is being kissed into your mouth on a warm summer night while the earth rises up to sing around you. You deserve to be touched the way that makes you feel like maybe your body, and all its painful losses, is just another bit of stardust. Maybe it's just the universe meeting itself in the shape of another, reaching out to touch them back and whisper, "*I've missed you.*"

Can you see yourself sitting in the sunlight, smelling like sunblock as the ocean caresses the shore beneath you? A sparkling drink in your hand, laughter easy on your lips, and someone who makes you feel like life's not so bad to toast your glass against? Can you see yourself spinning until you're dizzy, barefoot on the grass, falling into the comfort of finally feeling whole?

You don't need to be afraid to be seen, afraid that someone will get close enough to confirm that you're not worth loving. If you keep believing that, you might die before you ever really get to live.

And this life is meant to give us the *chance*. The chance to rise to the occasion, to grow, to learn, to fuck up, to say you're sorry. It can't be true that you're only allowed those beautiful moments if you are X amount of pounds. If your skin is clear. If your hair is shiny. You deserve a Christmas morning in matching pajamas. You deserve to be in pictures with your nieces and nephews so they can point at the photos when they're older and say, "Auntie! You were so beautiful!" You deserve to be in the pictures.

You deserve the big adventure—to be on the back of a beautiful boy's moped, or a gorgeous girl's Harley, and to laugh into the rain as lightning streaks the sky. You deserve the stories of diarrhea after a bad clam on a faraway beach. You should be able to smile as you remember the night you danced out of your heels in a club in the city, or the time you got on a bus in the wrong direction, or the time you met a beautiful lover with tumbling curls who was reading your favorite book in a coffee shop.

You should have good hookup stories, and bad hookup stories, and stories of running wild with girlfriends late into the night while some old biddy[8] shook her old biddy head at your reckless joy. You deserve to worry the church ladies, and to wear something that makes a cool-looking teenage girl say, *no, you're cool*,[9] and to walk holes into the soles of your shoes from all the places you've wandered.

It might not feel like it, but the life that I'm describing is happening right now for you. Right next to you. It's one lane over, just waiting for you to merge. All you have to do is change lanes. You can change your perspective. Throw on that blinker,

8. Being old is awesome, unless you're an old biddy who judges other women, then you're an old biddy.
9. The ultimate achievement.

and shift over. You can go slow, or you can Tokyo Drift that shit, but you have to cross the barrier to shift the way you see yourself. Take your life off of cruise control, and start driving like you mean it. Cruise control doesn't suit you anymore.

Maybe you are feeling a little resistant. It feels scary to hope, and even scarier to believe. While I suppose you could keep waiting until you somehow earn the right to be worthy, it will only be a waste of your precious, ticking time. As long as you keep thinking you have to change first, you'll always feel like the girl who doesn't deserve love. You'll feel that way until you *decide* that you don't want to feel like that anymore.

So please, for the love of your one, brief, exquisite, painful, colorful, stardust life—let it go. Let the fantasy version of you fade away, and let yourself be whole in the body you're living in. Let yourself believe there's a world where you're the main character, exactly as you are. Change lanes.

It might not feel like it now, but you're the only one who can stop you.

You're the only one who can stop you.

I'll see you in the sunshine, toasting and laughing and knowing you deserve it all.

Haunted Hallways

Of course I believe in ghosts—
don't you know how many hallways my heart still wanders
    through?

So I burn candles—
pile wildflowers, cloves
and crunchy fall leaves
together in the sunlight

then whisper:

Come back to me?

And sometimes, I swear I see her,
out of the corner of my eye,

but she is haunting empty hallways.
She never learned to say *goodbye.*

my roommate's
mother's ghost

This is a ghost story.

It was my first time living off campus during college. I packed my purple Scion xB[1] and drove to my college town to move in with a handful of other twenty-year-old "women."[2] We had scored a house with tons of space, a backyard, and I got my own bathroom. I was ecstatic to get there and move in.

My roommate, Hayley, had been living in the house mostly alone during the summer. Her boyfriend was the only other person who had been around. Their shameful sleepovers had occasionally livened up an otherwise lonely, hot season for Hayley.

This might be a good time to tell you: we were all fitfully, pitifully, and dutifully *in love with Jesus*. Not an average-Christian-gal-just-bumping-through-life-without-a-care-in-the-world sort of into Jesus. We were more like forsake-your-fleshy-sinful-body-lest-ye-burn-ye-nasty-harlot devoted to Jesus. The boyfriend

1. That's Alexander the Grape to you.
2. Spoiler alert: young-twenties people are often just kids with debit cards and attitude problems who think they don't have a goddamn thing to learn.

sleepovers were a secret, scandalous summer affair. She was risking becoming an outcast, but that was about to end! I was coming back!

I pulled into our driveway buzzing to see my buddy after being away so long. I strolled through the door, clad in Target yoga pants, Costco Ugg knockoffs, and a college logo sweatshirt, to find Hayley practically levitating with joy at my arrival. She threw her arms around me and said, "I'm *so* glad you're here!" Something about her voice rang a tiny alarm bell in my head. Hayley was *never* that excited to see . . . anyone. In a room full of chattering people, you might find her perched on the arm of a sofa, hawkeyed and carving off chunks of an apple with a switchblade. She had serious Katniss Everdeen vibes. But the little alarm I felt gave way to the much louder boom of my ego. Of *course* she missed me. After all, I was the Fun One.[3] Poor thing . . . in a house alone with only her boyfriend to keep her company. *Sad*, really.[4]

I plopped on the couch as Hayley and I began to catch up on what we'd missed since June. The blinds on the window next to the door were swinging in the gust from us slamming it closed behind us, and the soft swoosh became the soothing background to our excited, twentysomething gossip. "She's dating WHO?" *Swoosh*. "They broke up?!" *Swoosh*. "I heard they *had sex* in his parents' cabin this summer." *Swoosh*. "We should pray for her."

We carried on like that, two birds chirping a whole world's worth of news at each other, for a long time before I realized the blinds were . . . still swaying? The door was long since closed,

3. This was an opinion held exclusively by me—in reality, the night I turned twenty-one I was marking the liquor bottles with Sharpie to make sure the underaged roommates weren't underaged sinning with *my* Wild Turkey.
4. It's important to know that I was *so incredibly Christian* I really didn't get the appeal of a house alone with your boyfriend for a summer. I blame the *Veggie Tales*.

no windows were open, and no air-conditioning was on.[5] Even weirder, the blinds weren't losing any momentum. They were swinging with the exact same amount of power. I felt like I was watching an exhausted mother endlessly push her sticky child on the swings so they wouldn't start eating wood chips.[6] I stopped mid-gossipy-sentence, cocked my head, and said, "Hales . . . the blinds are still swinging. That's weird, right?"

Hayley gave me a very quick, very tight look before she jumped up from the couch and quickly mumbled, "Oh, yeah, I guess. I didn't notice." She was already pulling one tattered, toe-holed Vans shoe on. "I'm gonna run to the store. See you later!"

A flash of skater shoes and a baseball tee, and she was gone. The door closed behind her, and the blinds swung slowly to a stop the way they should have before.

Peculiar, no?

The rest of the roomies arrived, one by one, over the next few days. The house was bustling with the over-the-top performance of adulthood that only almost-adults can pull off. A couch with the stuffing poking through the fabric welcomed guests to our home. We crowded the walls with wooden signs covered in scripty Bible verses, photos from high school, and little bits and bobs we'd collected on travels and in other phases of life. A fresh, sparkly Vitamix blender (we had a couple of Smoothie Girls in the club) held court above a silverware drawer which would have made a matchy-matchy person fling themselves from the lido deck of a cruise ship. We even had one of those rare color-changing spoons you got in '90s cereal boxes.

---

5. My roommates and I fundamentally disagreed on if air-conditioning was a luxury or necessity. I usually lost, and I was usually sporting a sweat mustache.
6. Kids are always sticky. Like, why are you coated in a sheen of jam, Tiny Tim? What is your fucking problem, you toddling petri dish?

Though, it was always "dirty" when I wanted to use it. I suspect this was intentional.[7]

Our home became a chaotic tribute to the colliding currents of *becoming*. A mosaic of the feeling of tension and freedom we all contend with while we grow up. One current pulls us toward adulthood, one tugs us backward toward childhood, and they pin us hard and fast until we're neck deep in the churning white water.

But we were having fun. We hung a hammock between two very depressed-looking palm trees in the backyard,[8] there was a black cat next door named Binx who escaped his home to sun himself on our driveway and meow to us the neighborhood news, and we had a spare converted half room[9] that we put a Nintendo 64 and a projector in for epic *Super Smash Bros* tournaments.[10] We felt untouchable and so sure of everything. Now all I'm sure of is how little we knew.

Occasionally the house would creak or crack, the way that houses made of wood and plaster do, but that sounded like a landlord problem, am I right?[11] Overall, we were living the dream.

---

7. Considering that I once left raw turkey in a big mixing bowl on the counter for three days because I got distracted halfway through making meatballs and forgot about it (shoutout to the undiagnosed ADHD), I understand their hesitancy to let me use something as precious as the '90s color-changing cereal spoon.

8. The Smoothie Girls, who were much thinner than me, took to the hammock with much more confidence. I didn't believe those palm trees had ever been with a fat girl before, and I wasn't about to be their first.

9. That's Spare Oom to you.

10. This, and not milkshakes, brought all the God-fearing boys to the yard.

11. These particular landlords expected us to mow the lawn and do extensive landscaping. Like, in what world are five twentysomething nincompoops going to prune your semiannuals or however the fuck you garden? Sure, we said we'd do it, but you gotta remember, I was gonna get my own bathroom. I would have said anything. We did not get our security deposit back. RIP the grass.

Until the attic.

It's about to get spooky, folks.

The attic door was in Hayley's bathroom, but the bulk of the empty space was directly above my bed. Now, I'm still not sure who was the first to notice it, because initially, we all kept it to ourselves, afraid to be the Unhinged Roommate. I can only tell you what I noticed, and how absolutely bonkers my reaction was.

According to pop culture, attics are much more prone to housing Satan and his lackeys than other common spaces. Like, if a ghost moves in, it's going straight to the attic to check out the acoustics—natural lighting be damned. As someone who watched many episodes of *A Haunting*, I knew about attics and their reputation as a hot place to be in the underworld.

In the beginning, it was random. A huge bang here, what sounded like someone dragging a full-blown sectional there,[12] and the kind of knocking and stomping that could only be described as "intelligent" bookending it all. Between my bulletproof cultural references, the swinging blinds from week one, and the undeniable sounds from above, I began to suspect that the attic might have been converted into a supernatural nightclub.

The women from my mom's side of the family are very sensitive to the supernatural. On separate occasions my aunt and I have both had to leave buildings, rooms, and spaces that carry the Very Icky Vibes, and my grandma sees her mother some nights. The one exception is my mom. She just watches *Ghost Adventures* and searches her photographs for orbs.[13] No matter

---

12. In my experience, supernatural beings LOVE to redecorate. Big MOM-COME-SEE-MY-ROOM-I-CHANGED-EVERYTHING!!! energy.

13. One of the activities my mom and I can always count on to bring us together is laughing our asses off at the antics of Zak Bagans in *Ghost Adventures*. We have an entire fanfic subplot in which Zak doms the hell out of his number two, Aaron. It's an absolute riot.

how she tries, she cannot seem to make a connection with ghost-ies and ghoulies. This is a fact she loudly laments and resents me for, as she would like nothing more than to photograph a "nice Victorian lady in a beautiful dress who stays long enough for a picture but who doesn't try to touch." Once while in a haunted castle, my mother made this request aloud, and my Irish friend burst out laughing and said, "Trying to order a ghost like it's on Amazon is the most American thing I've ever heard." I, on the other hand, don't need a supernatural wish list. I have always been hypersensitive to negative energy entering a room. It's just another thing she and I cannot understand about each other.

The attic was haunted, and I was unmoved. It would have to do more than a couple stippy stomps and swingy swings to get my modest panties in a wad, so I slept peacefully under the rolling thunder above my bed and didn't give a single holy shit. I was used to finding pockets of normality while chaos tore through other rooms. I'd been doing that since I was just a little kid. Plus, I'd survived everything so far, so why let *this* bigger-than-me-with-a-bad-attitude thing *actually* scare me? I was a child of God. Some might call me reckless, but I say they lack imagination. After all, if God was for me, what kind of demon was gonna play grab-ass at 3:00 a.m. in my big, grown-up girl house? None that I'd heard of.

Fuck the confidence of a mediocre white man. Try the con-fidence of a mediocre white Christian woman who thinks there's a demon watching her sleep. You'll go places.

But pride cometh before the fall, and my pride just hurt its feelings. When I didn't give it the time of day, its behavior escalated. Once a throw pillow next to me began to levitate. An-other time my hair started blowing like someone was breathing directly on my face, and I smelled a breath like death. It lasted for five minutes while I refused to turn my head. Blinds swung and attics stomped and the air felt too heavy, like a blanket had been thrown over the house, but we still didn't talk about it.

I got home from classes one night after the sun had already set and walked to the front door in the half-there blue moonlight. I was the first home for the evening, and the house was pitch black inside and completely empty. As I slid my key into the lock, I heard every door in that fucking house slam shut at once. *Nope.*

I ran back to my car and called my friend Rick, a similarly delusional human puppy with huge paws and wide shoulders, and asked him to come go through the house with me, just to make sure "no one was inside."[14] He arrived ten minutes later wielding a comically large butcher knife glinting under the gentle moon. I spiritually rolled my eyes and thought, *Oh good, that'll stop it.* But I said, "Oh good! That'll stop him!"

I opened the door and we tentatively stepped inside, trying not to make a sound in case the would-be burglar was still in there,[15] and we could get the jump on him. We went through the house room by room until we found ourselves staring down the dark hallway toward the door to Hayley's room. We both hesitated, a shared chill rattling our teeth—because that room, to be quite frank, had Very Icky Vibes. I'd never mentioned these Very Icky Vibes to Rick, but Rick was a vibe man. Rick could tell.

We girded our collective loins as Rick turned the handle on the door to the master bedroom and slid it open against the too-plush carpet. It was the kind of door you had to push harder than you should have. Like the air inside it was too heavy to

---

14. Did I tell him I suspected the Devil's doing? No, he wouldn't have come, and Mama needed to go to bed ASAP. Mama was tired.

15. Clearly after the RARE '90s cereal spoon, which are selling for ten to fifteen bucks on Electronic Bay dot com at the time of this recording.

move without some extra conviction. The room beyond was an unnatural black, drenched in the sort of inkiness that swallows the shapes within, and I swear I heard Rick swallow (or was it me?) as we stepped onto the carpet.

In that instant, the kitchen exploded with sound.

We ran back across the house, abandoning Hayley's room, ready to catch a thief in the act, who surely would have been no match for two ding-dongs, a butcher knife, and the Holy Spirit. We threw the light switch. We froze.

Every cabinet and drawer in the kitchen was flung wide, drawn out, and gaping at us. A million empty eyes and open mouths, all poised in a silent scream.

Am I being dramatic? Sorry, but what the *fuck*, right?

Staring at the supernatural carnage, I *officially* gave a shit.

We weren't sure what to do, so we did the only thing you really can do when confronted with a problem which you have very little control over and which might make you lose your marbles if you think about it too much: we minimized that ish, *hard*. You know in a movie when a child bursts into a room where adults are doing something very adult? Or their dad has just punched a hole in the wall? Or their mom is sobbing on the floor, clutching a wedding photo to her chest, while her husband is off in the apartment of a woman who doesn't have any children to look after? And upon seeing it, the child just freezes, or backs out, or picks up the bottles their mom knocked off the nightstand when she slid down the wall in despair, and tries to make life feel normal again? That was Rick and me in the kitchen. We sort of quietly put things back together, cradling our fear in our arms, and wondering aloud if it was safe to go home yet, just like children who aren't sure how to handle something they can't understand. What else can you do in a moment like that?

Not long after the Door Slammy Slammy night, in the middle of an average Saturday, all of us were home doing our own thing when the evil attic nightclub popped off. It normally reserved activity for late at night, so I was shocked to hear it in broad daylight. For probably five minutes I listened alone in my room pretending not to hear the bass getting louder, until I finally squeaked my door open and slid out real sneaky-like to find my roommates slinking into the living room too. The last roommate, who had been in the shower directly under the epicenter of the current attic meltdown, emerged with soapy hair and wrapped in a towel. Despite having just been boiling under the kind of hot water only college girls can endure, she looked pale. She looked like she'd seen a ghost.

Finally, I said, "Do you all . . . hear that?"

One by one, we admitted that we'd been hearing the dragging, slamming, and stomping from the attic for weeks. Some of us had seen doors slam, some of us had seen things move, and some of us had woken up with strange bruises that looked a lot like teeth, but nothing like human ones. There were stories of beds levitating and of things disappearing to appear somewhere impossible. We tried to pin down when it had begun, searching for some sort of reason.

Hayley, quiet for most of the conversation, cleared her throat and said, "It's been happening since before any of you were here. Since summer. It's been here since I moved in."

I'm sorry . . . *what?*

"Why didn't you say anything?!" I demanded, thinking we could have saved a lot of time if she'd just owned up to the haunted house thing that day the blinds wouldn't stop swinging.

Hayley wouldn't meet my eyes as she muttered, "I didn't want to freak you guys out."

We were, officially, freaked out.

We had our landlords send an exterminator, a plumber, and a whatever-else-er to find the steel-toed raccoon family, electrical fuckery, or shit-clogged pipe that had been turning us into superstitious puritans who were prone to a fear of black goats. Every expert came, saw, and told us the same thing: There's nothing up there, and there's nothing wrong. It's not the pipes, it's not the wires, it's not the local fauna. No one knew where it was coming from—this tormenting chaos and noise that was hovering over a house full of girls doing their best to become women.

So we did what you have to when an unnamed evil entity is living rent-free in your house and mind—we ignored it. We didn't talk about it. We started sleeping with the lights on and over in each other's rooms. The ones with boyfriends endured the vicious whisper network of Christian gossip to stay over at their boys' houses. I fell asleep on the couch watching *The Office* a lot, and I turned the sleep timer off on the TV. In other words, we adjusted. We coped. We were trying to graduate college and fall in love and decide if we'd be missionaries or moms or the sort of sunny wife who bakes when we got out of there. We might have been haunted, but we were also very busy.

Some of us were faring better than others. Hayley was going on longer and longer runs, though the skin under her eyes was looking pretty dark. One of us was doing an elimination diet to control every single thing going into her body and chirping about how great she felt, but her face looked a lot like it might be made of porcelain—like the wrong question might send a crack right through her. The one who shared a room with Hayley wasn't sleeping, and she was starting to look brittle, like ash holding its shape before it's touched and blown away.

If you'd asked me, I would have told you that I was fine, really. I'd already spent a lot of my life living in a house with a negative mass of energy swirling around me. I was used to carrying on and building pockets of normalcy into the rotting wood. I took pride in not needing anyone to get rid of the thing in the attic for me. After all, no one ever had before. In other words, I wasn't doing very well either.

One night, under the sounds of something big and dark roiling twelve feet above me, Hayley snuck into my room and asked if we could talk. She perched on the edge of my bed, muscles tense. She reminded me of a deer when it hears a twig snap—alert and ready to run.

Then she took a deep breath and told me the truth.

We weren't haunted—*she* was.

Now, I ask you, Dear Reader, what the fuck was I supposed to say to that? Anyone have a handbook on "How to Stay Chill When Your Roommate Tells You She's Personally Haunted?" No? Okay, so with that in mind, I said,

"And you didn't think to mention this *before* we signed a lease!?"

Was this my best moment? No, but I am a practical, problem-solving type. I like personal accountability, and things being fair, and people being honest. I resented spending months assuming this was my problem, when really, it was *her* goddamned ghost.

"I . . . it's never been this *bad* before. I didn't think you'd notice."

She didn't think *I'd notice?* Me, who had seen at least five scary movies? Me, who considered myself extraordinary at *noticing stuff?* Once I was rear-ended in a Chipotle parking lot, and as I got out to exchange info, the girl peeled away and *flipped me off* out the window. But sucks to suck, burrito bitch, because I had just binged all of BBC's *Sherlock* and my observational skills were *sharp*. I got the make, model, year, color, and license plate. Case *closed*.

I put aside my indignation (and internally patted myself on the back for being such a saint) to ask the next logical question: "What, exactly, do you *mean* you're haunted?"

Hayley went on to tell me the story of her mother's mother's curse. How every woman from her mother's side of the family, going back as far as anyone was willing to say, had spent their life growing old with the Thing in Our Attic. Someone way back when made a bad deal, or killed the wrong man, or broke the wrong woman's heart, and ended up giving something dark and hungry an intergenerational piggyback ride. It was passed from daughter to daughter like a ring that kept reappearing in a jewelry box, no matter how many of them tried to throw it into the ocean.

Her mother never told Hayley the details of her cursed inheritance, but Hayley's older sister had started encountering the nighttime visitor at a very young age. She would greet a friend at the end of the bed who told her *he was hungry*. Every night she would rise around 3:00 a.m., get an apple from the kitchen, and return to her room. When she woke it would be on her nightstand, shiny and red, with a perfect, inhuman bite in the center.

Hayley had of course seen the signs of the haunting as a child—the sort of stories you tell around a campfire. But those were hot and fast and burning things that carve out a space in a child's mind and secure their place as tentpole memories. The more subtle, consistent ways it kept her company weren't noticeable until high school. And here, on the crest of adulthood, while we grappled with who we were if we weren't who we'd always been, it had peaked.

Knowing that the thing in the attic wasn't there for *us* did lift a bit of the daily stress. It was almost the end of the year, and Hayley had taken to rarely being home where her visitor would make itself known. We rode out the rest of school, and she made plans to move out as soon as she finished her last final.[16] We were the first house on the block to be empty for summer.

The next year, Hayley moved into a new house with no attic, and the club in ours was officially shut down. I lived another year in that house, and we never encountered levitating pillows or slamming cabinets again. Hayley had taken the attic dweller with her, but a funny thing happened: the air never quite felt *right*. For reasons no one can really remember, tensions flared, cruel words were spoken, and friendships met messy ends. I figured it had to be the house. The house and the echoes left behind by someone else's problems.

But I never stopped feeling haunted. I saw things out of the corner of my eye, but I could never pin them down. I would be somewhere new, with new people, and everything would be great—then I'd hear the first thudding step in the proverbial attic. A shiver would run through me, and I'd start looking around accusingly. Who brought the ghost this time? Who is about to turn this air between us toxic? Who can I blame for having to move out of another place where my heart had finally started to feel at home?

I couldn't see that the haunting thing was always hovering over my own shoulder. I was more like my mom than I realized.

Five years after we'd all graduated and moved away, the original roommates of the haunted house met in Palm Springs for a bachelorette party. I was a raw nerve, midtwenties and held together by duct tape and string. When I stepped out of the air-conditioned car into the merciless desert air, I was deep in the heart of realizing that every decision I'd made had been, on some level, a reaction to my mother. Isn't it funny how often

---

16. We didn't ask her to do this. She wanted to.

it comes back to that for girls? We are trying to earn their love, or replace their love, or be nothing like them at all. Just like our moms wanted to be nothing like theirs. Just like our grandmothers wanted to be nothing like theirs, either.

On days when I woke up feeling brave, I took a hard look at the choices I had made and thought, "*Oh shit, who am I if I'm not reacting to my family? Am I anyone at all?*" On days that I didn't feel brave, I carried on and coped, ignoring the sounds in my head. The sounds from the attic. I was learning how to identify the voices I'd inherited whispering deep under my own. I was getting better at unexpectedly seeing someone else in the mirror without flinching. There in the desert, I found myself in the unrelenting thick of heat and healing. I was getting better.

As we got ready for dinner and Hayley and I met again under the light of a hotel bathroom mirror, I felt a curious sting. Should I apologize to her for demanding she reveal her messy inheritance to me before she was ready? Should I tell her I finally understood why she couldn't name it until she could?

I hadn't seen her like this since we'd lived in the house with swinging blinds. It was so good to be together again, and we fell back into banter as if no time had passed at all.[17] As we winged our eyeliner and prepared to spend an evening in public with blinking penises on our heads, the bathroom lights flared, flickered, and plunged us into darkness. We waited for a beat in silence, and they came back on with a hum. Hayley didn't flinch. The skin under her eyes looked bright and even.

"So that's still happening, huh?" I asked casually, tugging lightly on the fabric of my dress. I applied a second coat of

---

17. There is no comfort quite like the company of someone who has gone through what you've gone through.

mascara that I knew wouldn't lengthen or curl my lashes after all these years, but I never gave up hope that I could change.

"Yep," she said with a shrug, as she straightened the stubborn ends of her hair, forcing nature to submit to her will.

And I know it sounds odd, but it didn't feel odd at all as we stood there under the familiar flickering light. We were just two old friends—two barely bloomed women at a bachelorette party. Two girls in a hotel bathroom, playing dress-up with our mothers' ghosts.

Such a Pretty Face

If this woman tells me I have *such a pretty face*,
specifically,
then talks about how "good" she's been
while ordering fruit as her side dish
instead of french fries?

I'll make her cry in a Corner Bakery.

we've been working for free & we don't even get dental

When I was growing up, our coffee table was constantly covered with a layer of *People*, *Us*, and *Today* magazines. My dad brought home the new *People* from the grocery store each week and offered it to my mom like a love letter. Her carry-on bag for flights was routinely stuffed full of enough magazines to fill a few hours. I would sit on the floor and listen as my mom and my grandma chattered away afternoons, gossiping about famous women they'd never met. "Who Wore It Best?" "What Was She Thinking?" "Stars—They're Just like Us!"

It was here, between the mothers in my family and the glossy, perfumed pages of celebrity gossip mags, that I learned how women talk about other women.

And friends, we need to talk about how we talk.

I've noticed something since I joined the world of social media and started sharing thoughts on the internet. If you are not a cis man, you learn quickly that there are rules.

Chief among them is this: you are not allowed to know, much less *say*, that you are attractive, hot, beautiful, or, above all, worthy. Worthy of what? Pretty much anything, but especially of love and attention from other lovely people.

If you violate this rule by suggesting that you might be nice to look at and inherently valuable, the churning mass of humanity will hurl forth its fierce protectors to tackle your ass into submission. There is no shortage of people with phones in their hands who feel invested in maintaining the status quo. They sense a threat to the Way Things Are and Have Always Been, and they rise up to crush you down to maintain homeostasis.

Now, we all know that a certain type of internet men (let's call them Keyboard Kens) thrive on telling women that they are fat,[1] ugly, and otherwise not something they want to consume. These are the cave dwellers who crawl into the light of a woman's comment section to type *"your not a 10 ur a 2 know ur place"* with their dirty fingernailed hands which have never touched a boobie, then retreat into the primordial sludge where they simmer in unoriginal resentment. We are all on the same page here, yeah? The Keyboard Kens are many, and they are largely forgettable.

I was prepared for the many Kens of the internet when I started sharing my life there, but I was caught off guard by their accomplices. Because it wasn't just the Keyboard Kens dropping in to remind me that grown men drinking Mountain Dew and scratching their meatballs in a basement somewhere didn't think I was pretty enough to be seen in public, it was *women.* So. Many. Women.

The first few clusters of hate comments from women left me shrugging my shoulders and thinking, "All right, the girls

---

1. I believe with my entire being that being fat is not a bad thing, I do not consider it an insult, but a neutral descriptor. For the sake of *this* conversation, I'm including it in the list of ways men attempt to insult women, because those men are aggressively fatphobic, and it is intended to put women back in their place.

are unwell, there must be a planet doing something dirty with an eclipse somewhere." But the more traction my stories got, the more consistent the phenomenon became. Any video that involved me referencing myself as attractive or dateable was met with a wave of backlash from both the crusty Kens and a reliable faction of woman-hating women.

Would most of those women proudly declare that they were misogynists? I doubt it. My grandma and mom wouldn't have said that they hated women while they picked apart the bodies and personhoods of others in magazine pages. The ones commenting on my appearance or presentation, eagerly attempting to socially police me back into a performance that falls in line with patriarchal scripts of women's roles, likely wouldn't say so either. Yet there they are, every single time I suggest I like myself and that someone else could too, to insist I shut up and get back into the internet's kitchen. I asked around and found much of the same—each gal I know who occupies the same social media creative space and likes themselves publicly has experienced it— if they cross the line established by a patriarchal society, women rise up to punish them.

What's that about? Why are we so willing to critique each other's appearance and behavior? To situate ourselves as more valuable than another because we look younger, thinner, paler, taller, etc.? We project the things we want to control and critique about *ourselves* onto each other. We believe our own intuition or moral compass is dictating what we declare is right or wrong, but in reality, we are regurgitating the poison that was shoved down our throats by those invested in keeping us subdued. We robotically enforce a social ladder: winners at the top, losers at the bottom—all kicking each other in the face to make sure we don't lose the high ground. So we must believe there is something up there that is a limited and critical resource. Does the top of the heap hold the key to power? Success? Safety? Will the growing pile of bodies beneath us with stiletto-shaped bruises on their faces give us access to the things men enjoy and keep and deny from others? Will enforcing the rules of acceptable womanhood as defined by men *really* give us the ability to walk through the night without wondering if we'll make it home?

Here's the part that really gets my proverbial goose:

We have nothing positive to show for our unconscious work on behalf of the patriarchy.

Insisting that women are thin hasn't resulted in us getting paid the same amount as men for identical labor. Suggesting that women are cocky or arrogant if they express an appreciation for themselves hasn't lowered the statistics around sexual assault. Coming to the defense of nameless men in the comments of a woman offering a valid critique of society hasn't gotten any gal's name written on the mysterious Girls to Not Be Shitty To list. There is no list. There is no club of elite women who Aren't like Other Girls and who get to have all the same things the men do. While it's true that women who do this policing and who perform womanhood in a way that makes boys hoot and holler are afforded *more* power and security than the women who don't, it's never going to be enough. At the end of the day, even the most One of the Guys girl is the first name on the list of expendable employees when budget cuts come to town.

Our propensity to enforce rigid standards for other women only benefits men. We uphold a social system that measures a woman's worth by measuring her efforts toward editing her natural self to fit into the ever-shifting outline of perfection and awards her with impossibly small tidbits of resources she should be entitled to in full as a human being. These bite-size aggressions are the bricks used to build the house they move so freely in, while we are locked in the basement. Men are allowed to hurt women because they built a world that lets them do so without consistent or serious consequences. The world where small, easily excusable things support the weight of larger, heavier transgressions. That world only keeps spinning if someone else is greasing the wheels for free. Something as simple as gossiping about our friends' weight gain directly contributes to the way men are empowered to be violent toward women. Without ever meaning to, we contribute to upholding their power over us.[2]

I get it. We all want to feel like we aren't vulnerable to the whims of cis men. We all want to feel safe. We all want to feel in control.

But we never get there. That's the whole point. We uphold a system that grinds us down into bloody nubs of who we could have been, and we do it in exchange for nothing at all. It's a full-time job with zero pay, and it doesn't even come with dental, girl. MEN ARE NOT PAYING US TO UPHOLD THEIR RULES AND BULLSHIT.

So, buddy, *don't work for fucking free.*

Imagine, for a minute, a world in which no one fucking cared what women looked like. Imagine a world where the older a woman looked, the more sought after she became. We would crave her wit, her wisdom, her sacred knowledge, her presence in her body, her mastery of self—following after her in the hope that we might learn from her valuable experience. Imagine a world in which there was no concept of *pretty.* Where men never sat in groups critiquing women's bodies, but rather, they sat in groups wondering at our brilliance. Imagine a world where there

---

2. I'm speaking in a monolith here, but it's critical to note that this is even more true for women and non-cis men of color. White women do this shit all the time, but we also benefit from it in terms of upholding Eurocentric beauty standards: a.k.a. white supremacy nonsense. We uphold not just men's power over us, we uphold our power over women of color.

was no competition to be chosen by the men who make us beg for our own safety. Imagine a world where women are believed.

What if your mother, or her mother, or her mother before her were sent to school and told to create and learn and invent. What if your mother's mother was given money and resources and a research lab with assistants, and she set her mind to finding a cure for cancer? Or hunger? Imagine if women had been allowed in science the way men had. Women's health would just be health and we wouldn't be suffering through shit like endometriosis, PCOS, and birthing mortality rates. This is even more true for women of color, who still suffer worse prognoses in the face of reproductive-health issues. What if there was a world where women were seen as equal to men, and no one thought about their appearance before their contributions, and no one believed they deserved to be a subcategory under the things that are given to men without qualification.

That world, of course, does not exist. And while there are many reasons for the absence of an equitable society, and the only people responsible for hurting others are the people choosing to hurt, a part of that world exists because those of us suffering under the imbalance are, as a group, occupied with consumability.

What if we all just embraced each other and told our friends, lovingly, to shut the fuck up when they mention another woman's cellulite?

Like a very cheery, "Whoops! I don't talk about other girls' bodies that way! It's not good for anyone!"

Or a, "Babes, we have much more important things to worry about than someone else's filler."

Or, my personal favorite: "If it makes them happy and they aren't hurting anyone, I really can't afford to give a fuck. I am very tired, and I'm craving cheese. Let's get cheese."

Tell your friends to keep you on the righteous path of Michelle Obama, Leslie Knope, Miss Patty,[3] Mama Cass, and Elle Woods. From now on, we only see women in terms of their limitless potential, we tell tall tales of our own grandeur, and we clap for each other's wild stories.

Let's be our own superheroes, with all the steely resilience of the Marvel boys wrapped into the softness of a grandmother's arms while she stirs a simmering pot. What if we blended the unyielding courage of the *Toy Story* gang with the pealing laughter of a group of twentysomethings going out-out in short dresses, despite the freezing cold? And what if when we saw those laughing girls, with their boobs still high and their hair still so shiny and their bodies still so fresh, we didn't think some nasty thing about how ridiculous they looked freezing their asses off? What if instead we remembered the day we were those girls, nostalgic for the wild laughter and the feeling of being so new, and we thought:

Wow. What a glorious, beautiful thing to behold. What a precious thing to be young and free with the whole night unfolding ahead of you. I hope for them the very best. I hope for them joy and safety and ease. I hope for them the whole world.

I believe there's a world in which we are the CEOs, the leaders, the scientists, and the decision makers, and most importantly, the compassionate listeners. There we think of each other fondly, and speak of each other highly, and listen when the folks who have suffered have something to say. We step down when we should. We do not covet power. We only covet peace—for everyone.

---

3. Miss Patty from *Gilmore Girls* is a fat icon in a severely fatphobic show. Her one-woman performance in which she talked about her "gams"? Incredible.

I believe there's a world in which the people who aren't cis men don't fear for their lives in the night. And I know it's not nearly as simple as this, but in that world, nobody's friend tells them that their favorite bathing suit isn't flattering their figure. What if we started radically rejecting the way things have been? A group of women behind a common cause is a fearsome thing to behold.

So let's get together and burn the celebrity gossip magazines in a righteous bonfire, and dance naked under the moonlight, all mud and sweat and shrieks, until the word gets out and we inspire new rumors of witches in the woods.

Let's do what we can to make a world of beauty, safety, and brilliance for everyone. Let's do what we can to make sure we all make it.

affirmations
for people just
doing their best

I'm not a fan of affirmations. All that touchy-feely makes me a little squirmy, even on my most self-compassionate days. On my less self-compassionate days, they feel both gross *and* unrealistic. Some days I just need a list of achievable, believable, slightly unhinged reminders that I'm not as garbage-filled as perhaps my brain is telling me. So the following is a list of affirmations for those of us with goblin brains who need something we can hold on to, but that won't make us nauseous.

1. I would look better in a powdered wig than a seventeenth-century assclown.
2. I am less annoying than spending all day in a very itchy sweater.
3. I look like my photos and do not look like a slack-jawed blobfish.
4. I am less awkward than watching a grown man crawl onto Santa's lap at the mall.
5. I could kick down a door better than a silly little SWAT team.

6. I am very sneaky and do not have the clomping gait of a canned-bean giant.

7. I control my emotions better than the angry ghost of a Republican congressman.

8. Some people would rather kiss my face than eat ice cream with a very big spoon.

9. I am a better listener than the screaming airplane baby.

10. I could steal the Declaration of Independence and I would never, ever get caught.

11. I have never been told that I look like a vacant-eyed buffalo.

12. I am God's favorite because the ghouls in the haunted house are scared of ME.

13. Netflix wants to be my friend so bad when it asks if I'm still watching.

14. No one has ever seen me coming and yelled, "Who is that shambling fish stick?"

15. When I send people funny little pictures they do not say, "No more, you flushless toilet!"

16. I have never gained or lost weight because gravity is fake news.

17. I smell much better than the putrid stink of tuna casserole in a pond.

18. I am good at my job and I've never been fired for forgetting my pants at home.

19. Hearing me sing is better than hearing the shriek of an old floaty banshee.

20. I have never, ever tackled a toddler like an impish garden cat.

21. I am doing better than a wealthy man whose podcast has just been canceled.

22. I would not be voted out first on a reality TV show.
23. There are still some good foods I can definitely digest.
24. I will clean out that one drawer full of mystery kerfuffle before I die an epic death.
25. I deserve quality shoes with decent arch support.

Satellites

Do you think satellites ever get lonely?
Loved by so many in a faraway sky?
We count on them to go first—
be bold and brave
and send the good stuff back to the rest of us.

I don't know what a satellite looks like up close, really.
It's just another star
forcing a trail
through a crowded night.

change is constant,
karen's on a vespa
& we need to get on board

I have suspected for a long time that the biggest secret no one tells you is that you never *really* feel done. You never really wake up and think, "I have nothing left to learn. I know the answers to all the questions. I am prepared for any- and everything. I am complete."

We measure our lives in milestones—counting down the big ones until we're fully grown up. A real adult—probably with a successful relationship, a well-paying job, a house. (And if you're a woman, you better have a child, or a damn good excuse not to.)

When the milestones run out, though, we're supposed to stop changing, especially if you're a woman. We are not supposed to keep shedding our skins, changing our belief systems and our circumstances and behavior. We are only given the allowance to make small, consumable shifts. How else will people look to you for comfort when *they* need it? Mothers are supposed to answer the phone in the same exact way every time. There is no event large enough that encourages us to embrace a complete do-over for a woman. Oh, Karen's husband fucked his scuba instructor and bought a sleazy time-share in Majorca?

Karen must be going through it. Karen should take up pottery, probably. Pottery would be *wild*.

But Karen doesn't get the same support when, after being confronted with the scuba-suit-clad siren and the dirty love nest, she sells her house and goes to Italy to ride on the back of twenty-five-year-old Giuseppe's Vespa, does she? Then Karen is crazy, and Karen is out of touch, and Karen has responsibilities she's just abandoning. Karen, it turns out, is a selfish, unhinged bitch. Can you believe she just left everyone behind?

No time-share for Karen.

That doesn't seem very fair, though, right? I mean, sometimes life just ends up that way for Karen, and Karen didn't even get a say in the home-wrecking mermaid or the bed of lies in Spain. Life can deal you a rancid hand so awful, your only option is to quit playing poker entirely and leave Las Vegas behind you. You have to wake up, decide you're sick of this shit, and end the day straddling a scooter in Tuscany. Sometimes life is like that. Sometimes, life is a brand-new page and a beautiful boy named Giuseppe.

What if women were allowed to do truly wild things? What if we let them dye their hair pink and take up pole dancing at forty-five, just because they want to try on someone new, the way they might try a bright nail polish color after years of wearing neutrals? What would the world look like if we decided not to whisper about the photo of Karen and her hot Giuseppe, and instead rallied behind her with curiosity?

Karen, how are you doing? Karen, what are you learning? Karen, how can I support you while you are living a life so unfamiliar? Karen, have you found someone new under those old layers of you? Karen, is that man as good in bed as he looks?

Change is scary—even when we see it in *other* people. Most of us, myself included, have a knee-jerk reaction to stop it when it comes on too fast and too strong and makes the stable women we know seem unrecognizable. Men have much more room, for much longer, to change. They are allowed to do erratic, spontaneous, and selfish things in pursuit of Becoming a Man. They are allowed to lure a fish-loving blond into their fish-loving beds and get rewarded with keynote speaking gigs and shit. *"Look at him going after what he wants! We could learn a thing or two from him!"*

But when women change—when they go full Leo on a yacht with model boyfriends and martinis before noon—we can't cope with that as easily, can we? We are affronted, and our little chests puff up, and we plant our feet to tsk, "Who is Change to bust into our lives and make our mothers and sisters and aunties suddenly look and sound so different? Who is Change to steal from us our comfort and consistency? Change cannot snatch me from the bosom! Aunt Karen looks so embarrassing on her icky rental Vespa."

I can't help but wonder, though, what would happen if we embraced the fact that, for women, *change* is one of the only things we can ever really count on.

I like to imagine our bookshelves and movie theaters stocked with stories of gals gone wild, trying on new selves and new lives as often or as rarely as they called to us, and all of them celebrated for their courage. Don't we deserve classic stories of the triumphant, not tragic, ways we always endure what we cannot control? I think specifically of the many ways women have to survive men and their choices. Men who make choices on our behalf. Men who leave or who lose or who hurt. So many stories of women as heroes are about them surviving what men hath wrought, and I wonder what it would be like to see a woman who was being heroic on her own terms. Because of her own choices.

I hope for all of us we have a moment of bravery and abandon like our friend Karen. Whether it will be something as visible as an Italian escape, or something as quietly revolutionary as breaking the chain of hurt that's been passed down through your family for as long as anyone can remember, I know that change will find us all at least once. It will kick down our door, snatch the remote from our hand, turn off our twentieth re-watch of *Fleabag*,[1] and demand we answer its question: *Do you have the courage to come with me?*

Deciding how we will answer the call of change is something we all have to do for ourselves. It's personal and it's complicated and there is always a lot to consider, but one of the hardest parts of change is one we should not *have* to consider. We are often forced to weigh the reactions of lots of *other* people.

It's a shame, but *we* are often the hardest part of each other's necessary growth, aren't we? It's so hard to accept, but our loved ones might be ready to change well before we're ready to let them go. And so we stand in the way, holding out our hurt feelings and disbelief, beckoning each other to take them on as a burden to bear. We ask, "How could they up and leave? What does that say about them? What does that say about *me*?"

As much as I love to encourage the gals to dig deep and follow the wild call of their hearts, I also understand the tender soreness that comes with it. And I know it's not always just the person who is evolving who feels the ache of things stretching and growing suddenly old. It's painful to feel left behind. We are all only human, after all.

So consider this an appeal to the abandon in us all, no

1. If you try to tell me that you don't have a thing for the Hot Priest, I'll tell you that you're a liar. I don't care who you are or what your sexual orientation is—the Hot Priest is above it all.

matter where we're sitting when Change comes to town. We may be the door it knocks on, or the loving neighbor, or the kid who thought their mom would stay the same forever. Let us be brave enough to embrace Change, wise enough to know when it's time, and kind enough to let each other grow when we need to find new soil. Kind enough to accept that sometimes Change will take away the women we love and transform them into something new and important. We can decide today, together, that women are allowed to never stop changing if they need to. We can be free to pursue the best version of ourselves, of our life, until the end.

After all, Karen's on a Vespa, not checking her phone or seeing any passive-aggressive text messages in her family group chat. And it's really none of their business anyway.

twenty-nine-year-three-hundred-and-sixty-four-day-and-twenty-two-hour-old virgin

I lost my virginity when I was exactly twenty-nine years, three hundred and sixty-four days, and twenty-two hours old. You read that right. At ten o'clock p.m., the night before my thirtieth birthday, I welcomed the presence of a man's secret sausage into my forbidden bun. He was tall, half Scottish and half Irish (like when you get a swirl cone because you can't choose between your two favorite flavors, but, like, man version), and he didn't hesitate at all when I said, "I want to lay back and do nothing—I just want to enjoy the moment and focus on myself." One second I was so nervous I was chugging champagne to get over the hump (heh, hump), and the next my feet were in the air and my soul had temporarily vacated my body. Disembodied-me was munchin' on popcorn and looking down at sheathing-the-highlander's-sword-me and being like, "Damn girl, way to manifest." I was in a massive suite overlooking the sparkling Edinburgh skyline, the hot things that get said were being said in a Scottish accent, and it was exactly what I wanted. When it was over, I was showered, robed, and had kicked him out to read my mystery stories by midnight. *Perfection.*

You might be thinking something like, *Holy shit, that's a really long time to be a virgin,* or maybe something even meaner like, *Wow, what is wrong with her?* And I get that, since I used to think that too. Every high school movie on the planet would suggest I'm a big loser freak show. Very few of us intrinsically question the truth behind the stories that are presented to us as fact. I definitely do not include myself in the group of people born with the fuck-it bone. Most of my life, I was a pitifully bound rule follower who really adored a status quo, and I didn't have a fuck-it bone in my body.

I loved a metric of success—a preestablished tool that you could hold your own life and performance against and be told, in no uncertain terms, where you fell in regard to excellence or failure. It was like candy to me. I was a straight-A student, a varsity athlete by age fifteen, a star church kid, and I had a ton of friends. Then I was summa cum laude and a member of, like, twenty honor societies; I was a leader in a large student organization; and I had a great job right out of college. Then I was getting my master's degree. Then I was succeeding in tech and marketing. Then I was suddenly thriving on social media. All the while, I was a card-carrying member of Super Weenie Hut Junior whose sex life could have inspired a Steve Carell comedy, or a new *Mummy* flick where they find a cursed tomb that's never been opened, and it haunted me. I told myself I didn't care about being a prime candidate for a pagan sacrifice at my late age, but the truth was I felt like there was something wrong with me. Despite the many opportunities I'd had to save a horse and ride a cowboy, and despite the fact that I did, indeed, *want* the glowing skin of a girl who's been properly plowed, I still couldn't bring myself to do it. I was definitely, *definitely* defective. Up until very shortly before the maiden voyage of my sweet little luxury cruise liner, I remained deeply fraught about my status as a hot-girl-Hunter-of-Artemis.[1]

So how did I go from Houdini-level vanishing acts whenever somebody wanted to touch me to adding one more glorious tale of lust and conquest to the long saga of Scotland's rich history? I'm excited to tell you.

Sex is something that every single woman is taught to understand as a key part of their identity. It is our value, our bargaining chip, and our secret to protect. We are set up to fail from every angle, expected to be both virginal and accessible, both sexual and chaste. We are told that having sex makes us easy and used, decreasing our value to men, while not having sex makes us ice-queen prudes who are shrewish and mean, decreasing our value to men. Sex is used to control us, it's used to categorize us, and it's often used to brutalize us in disgusting expressions of power. Sex is important and intrinsic. There is no womanhood without sex. There is no girlhood without sex. We are sexualized from the day we are born until the day we die, and there is very little exception.

If we want to be a success, to be valued and worthy, we have to be sexy. When I was growing up, being sexy meant being thin.

I was not thin. Not by the standards I was being held against.

It was a metric of success that I was constantly falling short of, which made me a blatant failure, visible to anyone who saw me. I couldn't even hide my shame. I was too big to take on a date with your head held high. It was my biggest failing and my biggest fear, this body. Everybody knew it.

And I was made aware of that.

---

1. The bad bitches who hunted with Artemis were sworn to reject all sex and romance for the rest of their lives. Think nuns with crossbows and a bone to pick.

When we fall outside the lines of prescribed behavior for our oppressed identities, we are inevitably subjected to pain and embarrassment until we fall back in line. So I was told by family, friends, and the boys I liked that I just needed to be a little bit thinner. The doctors told my parents my weight needed to be controlled, the way every doctor told every parent of every fat child in the nineties and noughties. I was on diets by the time I was eight years old—the same year I learned multiplication and brought my dog to class for show and tell. Boys who secretly messaged me at night to talk for hours called me cruel names at school. I was forced into exercise, and my meals were watched by every adult in my life.

In high school, I was told by popular boys that I'd be hot if I only had a better ass or a thinner stomach. They said I was *so close* to finally being someone that could be loved out loud. I was made to work a little longer than other girls at volleyball practice. I snuck into the teachers' rooms to heat up my prepackaged diet food I brought for lunch. The boy I wanted so badly to love me back offered to work out with me, and he only took me places in public after I'd completed a particularly vicious diet and was thin enough to seem like I belonged beside him. It didn't matter that in almost every other way, we really felt like soulmates. My body wasn't right, so neither were we.

I was reminded, again and again, that the main obstacle to my success as a girl was the grotesque softness of my body. Not because I suffered in health or in ability. I was simply falling short of the standard of beauty. If I wanted to be deemed as worthy, men needed to want to fuck me *and* introduce me to their mother afterward. That wasn't happening.

So I gravitated to men who didn't want my body, but would take the rest. I filled my life with other things, and I accomplished a ton, and I made my résumé all but bulletproof. In every single way but sex, I was confident and at the top of my game. I worked so hard to disguise my failure to have a *good* body by having the best of everything else, and I didn't let anyone close enough to see through the disguise to the unlovable girl within.

I counted calories and exercised until I saw spots, all the while draping myself in fabrics that didn't cling and always being busy when friends had pool parties. As long as no one saw me, *touched* me, I could keep my distance while I tried to lose weight. I could function in the realm of "in progress." But the minute that a boy touched me and could see how fat I really was, was the minute it was all over. If I ever got found out for being bigger than I looked, I'd be immediately cast into the land of rejects, and I'd never get out. I would be expelled from the school of womanhood.

It felt like sex wasn't meant for me until I was thin. I'd never even seen a sex scene with a body that looked like mine, which meant none of the boys I'd be sleeping with had either. They'd have to be one of those super-advanced I-don't-care-what-anyone-thinks-I-love-your-body types, and those really didn't exist. What boy did I know who wouldn't care if his mom fat-shamed me when he brought me home to meet the parents? No one. That's who. That boy wasn't real.

By the time I was a grown woman and should have been empowered in my sexuality, I was still guarding the secret of exactly what I looked like naked like it could bring my entire world down around me. What if someone saw me and pulled back, disgusted? What if he rejected me? What if he confirmed the very worst fear I had about myself—that my body made me fundamentally unlovable—and then I couldn't even *pretend* that wasn't true anymore? What if I was going to be locked out of belonging forever?

I spent years worrying about what to do and what not to

do, but I wasn't getting anywhere, and it started costing too much of my energy. As I learned to deconstruct other parts of my life, my fear that my body was the worst thing about me and a secret I needed to hide started to fade. Other things in my life had started to need my attention. I went through a lot of loss, and my perspective on life changed. I didn't have the resources to care about "sexiness" anymore, and I was starting to not care about what anyone thought of me at all. When I learned that I deserved to be treated better than I had been by the people whose love I craved the most, the distance between us grew, and I stopped caring as much about what they thought of me. I wasn't afraid the boy I'd loved would touch me the wrong way and feel repulsed. I was exhausted, and eventually, I just had to let it go. I decided I was done telling men who wanted me that they were wrong to do so, or telling men that wanted every *other* part of me that they were right to do so, or shutting down my own chances at pleasure and self-discovery before they were even at the door.

I was about to turn thirty, I had a lot of life ahead of me, and what was the worst that could happen? I get rejected by some dude I might never see again? I mean, okay. I'd been through worse. I'd been rejected by people that actually mattered to me, and I'd survived it. I just wanted to live a good life. I just wanted to give myself everything I'd always been denied.

That's how I ended up in a Scottish hotel room putting all my fears to bed.

In the wake of my vahooganah's red carpet debut, it became pretty clear pretty quickly that all my angst had been for nothing. The ways that I'd hidden myself to avoid the crushing blow of rejection and abandonment over my soft body had been a waste. All those rules and social scripts about who, when, and how you should be fucking? They were a waste of time. I'd spent so much time and energy worrying that I was behind, that I was some sort of reject and freak and that everyone was slipping pickles and hiding corncobs but me. I'd been so well convinced no one would want me until I changed, I'd turned to rejecting myself before anyone else had the chance to.

If there had been some wave of opposition, a great collection of friends, pop culture, and loved ones who had heard my fears and told me I was wrong, that I was not too big or too old or too strange to be sexual, I might have believed it. When I did express my fears or searched the media for proof that I wasn't a strange fluke of evolution who repulsed potential mates, I didn't get much to prove me wrong. There was a gap between the messages I received about my worth and the truth between the sheets. In my twenty-nine years, I'd turned down more propositions than I could count, but so rarely by people who wanted to love me out loud. The dirty secret is that a lot of those people who told me to change but who wanted me in the dark were afraid to be different, too, so they toed the company line.

There are a ton of people out there who aren't having sex. There are a lot of people who are thirtysomething and older who haven't, or who have only had sex with one or two people, and who don't really identify with Carrie Bradshaw and her pals. But there are also people that do, and who fight the uphill battle of being sexually fulfilled without being branded as dirty and cheapened. There are plenty of people who want to live their best Samantha life. Fat people have sex, and thin people have sex. Old and young, disabled and able-bodied, religious and atheist—everyone does. *And* everyone doesn't. There really aren't any hard-and-fast rules.

Sex and our experiences with it are not an accurate metric we can use to measure our value and success as people. There is no right way to have or not have sex outside of basic things like consent and safety and honoring boundaries. You can have as much sex or as little sex as you want. You can fuck friends or lovers or strangers. You can be in love and never touch. You can not want sex at all, you can only want sex and no love, you can go twenty years between partners, and you can fuck someone new every night.

There isn't a "normal" way for people to experience sex. There isn't a "normal" age. There is no "normal" body or "normal" pairing. The only thing true for all of us is that we are crushed under the thumb of the cultural scripts surrounding sexuality, success, and value. We impose them on ourselves, and we impose them on each other. Those scripts, of course, serve to control people and make them feel scared about violating the terms and conditions for the way things are.

I believed them, and I lived it, and then I let it go. As I lay starfish-style in my king-sized bed, minutes from thirty and reflecting on the loss of my virginity,[2] I wondered if I felt any different. Had the many years of suffering and self-denial kept me safe from some great ego death after someone saw me naked? Nope. I was the exact same hot, smart, funny, successful bitch I'd been before I had a wizard staff in my cave of wonders, and I'd be that bitch forever. I didn't feel any more or any less. I didn't feel validated or like I'd found a part of me that had been missing. All those people who had given me notes on how to edit my body to be a success were completely full of shit. I only felt like a true hero for being bubble-bath-soft and expensive-champagne-buzzed while I doodled a bonnie Scot's noodle.

---

2. A concept I don't believe in, by the way. Virginity is a fun way to say, "No one has purchased her yet! You still can own this vagina!" And that's some fucking bullshit. So virginity is not a thing, babes.

In truth, I'm not even sure if I would have done anything differently had I never been told that my body was unworthy. Even in a perfect world, I might not have met anyone I wanted to have sex with. I might not have wanted to have sex with the people who wanted to have sex with me. I might not have wanted to have sex at all. And I would have been just as valuable and deserving.

Our sex and sexuality and bodies are our own. There is no such thing as a better body making someone a better person. There are no rules set besides the ones we set for ourselves. Even if someone says it to your face, all bold and ridiculous, you should know they're full of it and you are not half-baked, waiting to turn into something delicious. You already are. And anyone who tells you otherwise, whether it be your first love or parent or teacher or president or favorite movie star or God himself, is a small-minded, weenie-headed mole rat.

Loose Hands

I am trying to learn to hold things with loose hands
instead of pressing red crescents into my palms,
suffocating the thing I am so desperate to keep,
wondering why it hurts so much to love.

I imagine you, now,
fragile and spinning like I'm catching a flower,
lowered into the swirling, babbling sort of water
that coaxes music from the black river rocks,

and I pray that you'll stay.

But if you dance through my fingers and are carried away
I imagine, now,
that you are simply
not meant to be mine.

I imagine, now,
That my hands might be,
can be,
empty

and perfectly *fine.*

so you auditioned for the leading lady & you got cast as the cow

If there's one thing in my life that I regret, in the big sort of Wow-I-Wish-I'd-Chosen-This-Life-Path-Instead-of-the-One-I-Did kind of way, it's not being a part of musical theater. I've been a dramatic, over-the-top, born to perform little grub since my first wriggle. One time I told my parents to watch me sing along with the entire Britney Spears album at like 7:00 p.m. on a work night, and when they said they didn't want to I burst into tears and ran to my room sobbing, "*Sorry I'm such a burden!*" My dad appeared in the doorway a few minutes later, bedraggled, and I made him beg me to sing it. I did the entire thing in a Barbie nightgown hiding behind the foot of my bed so he couldn't see me—he just had to stand in the hallway and listen. *See?*

Instead of musical theater, I ended up in athletics. My dad played volleyball, and so did I. I learned a lot there, I had great quality time with my dad bonding over one of his greatest loves, and I met lifelong friends—but I was never meant to be Troy Bolton. I wasn't meant to have one foot on the court and one on the stage. I overheated in the sun, I had to have cold drinks to get through practice without collapsing, and I missed the

first conditioning session of the year because I'd gotten so badly
sunburned the day before I was home lying naked in bed crying
while my mother and grandmother dragged cold tea bags over
my back. I wasn't built for the life of an Olympian.

Some responsible adult probably should have tried to tell
me, because you couldn't *not* see it. One look at me and you
know I'm built to be a tavern minstrel, not a long-distance
hunter. I should have a bosom just tumbling out of the top of
an apron. Men listening to my songs should be asking me to
sing them lullabies, tell them a story, and pour them another
pint. I've said it once and I'll say it twice, I'm like fifty percent
potato. I should know every way to *cook* a potato. I should be
hustling travelers who think they're hot shit in pool as they
pass through my pub on their way to an epic quest to fight a
giant spider or dragon or kiss an ogre.[1] I should be telling stories around a fire and singing the emotional, big-chested solo.

I cannot watch a musical without bursting into tears.[2] I also
weep inconsolably when I watch *The Voice* auditions, or *So You
Think You Can Dance* auditions. There's something so exqui-
sitely human about people being brave enough to lay themselves
bare in front of someone they respect and stand there, waiting
to hear if they were *good enough*. They did the best they could,
they tried to say exactly who they were and why they deserved a
place in the world, and now they hold their heart outstretched
in their hands—waiting for it to bloom in the warmth of acceptance, or turn brittle in rejection.

Now, not all of us have tried to pull off the Kelly Clarkson

---

1. If I were a fantasy book character I'd either be the dark, mysterious,
knife-throwing side character who you can't tell is good or evil, or one hundred
percent the loveable, tavern-owning fat woman. There is no in-between.

2. You hit me with a high note? I'm weeping. You hit me with an emotional midshow anthem from the empathetic side character who doesn't get the
love story? Call an ambulance.

special, but we have all been onstage. We write, direct, and perform the stories of our lives, finding ways to say who we are and where we belong. We decide what to tell and who to invite to the play. Making sense of the world is hard and beautiful work. We go out and experience everything being human has to throw at us, then we retreat into ourselves to turn it into art—to situate the things we've survived or the things we've accomplished in a larger narrative about why and how. When we are ready, we step into the spotlight as the main character, and we do our best to make sure that the people who witness us leave knowing who we are. We want them to know why we have done what we have and gone where we've gone and said what we've said. As the plot unfolds before us, we can rewrite our pages to reflect things that have changed or to reflect how *we* have changed. Some characters are written out, some turn into lovers or villains, and some stay exactly the same. In the daily performance of our unique tales, we are the main characters and creators, and all the world's a stage.

No one can take our place as the star, so we audition everyone who we come to know for the supporting roles in our cast. We choose who will play our friends, our enemies, our monsters and lovers, and who will make it from Act I all the way to the end. But there are billions of people taking the stage on their own every night, starring in a completely different story than ours, and those people are casting their supporting cast, too. While we have control over what kind of person we play in the picture we paint, we are at the mercy of a different director and playwright when we audition to be in other people's lives. We may see ourselves as a perfect fit for the romantic lead or the conquering champion, give an audition that would make Barbra Streisand weep, only to giddily trace our fingers down the casting sheet and find our name written next to . . . THE COW.

I wasn't a theater kid, but I have wear-my-pajamas-to-school energy, so I have a lot of theater-kid friends. They've been in a hundred different plays, sang a hundred different songs, and auditioned thousands of times, but one thing is almost always the same: plus-sized girls, no matter how talented, deserving, or beautiful, get cast as the proverbial cow. Or the grandma. Maybe mother. Hearty animal sidekick or plump family friend. But they are never, in a million, billion years, landing the female lead. Despite claiming to be fair and honest in their casting, the world of theater continues to refuse to cast fat women in the roles their auditions should have earned.

We can all experience a similar frustration when we are cast by the people we know. We might be gleefully supportive, show up with soup when they're sick, and always answer the phone when they call, then feel like we've gotten the wind knocked out of us when we find out we've been cast as the villain. Perhaps we leave our whole heart on the stage performing the solo number given to the role of Good Child, but find out we'll be playing the Screwup. In our own story, we can be sure that our character rings true, but on anyone else's stage and to their rapt audience? We're completely at their mercy.

When we really love someone and get miscast, it hurts so much more. We want their respect, or their love, or for them to understand us, so we really prepare for our audition to land our perfect role. We throw ourselves into showing up in their lives as the people we want to be, and when the last note rings out we're rocking jazz hands, panting and exhausted, waiting for them to say we got the part. The moment they tell us they don't think we're a good fit, but we're perfect for *another* character we don't resonate with at all, can crush us. It feels personal. So we get angry, or we get devastated, or we insist we get another chance to prove they're wrong about us. But we're not the ones writing that story, and there are probably things we don't know.

Sometimes the role we think is perfect for us has already been given to somebody else. Sometimes the person writing the story has a specific type of person in mind for the character you want, or has a specific way they want the story to end. Casting us in the part we are sure we deserve could mean having to re-write the main character, or changing the way they are planning to act, and that's not something most writers are willing to do. Once someone has decided they're the good guy or the hero, they might change everything else to make that true. We might stumble into their open audition after they've already decided the main character will be the victim of someone terrible, and they've filled every other role.

The stories people tell about us often have very little to do with who we actually are. They look at their own life and who they have become, and they write an explanation that makes it okay. No one is ready to be honest about themselves one hundred percent of the time. It usually takes people a minute to see themselves clearly when they feel hurt, or angry, or scared. Some people never see themselves clearly at all, content to protect their self-image with a wild tale of fiction. How somebody else decides to understand us is usually all about them, and not a reflection of who we are or which role in their story we believe we have earned. Some people cannot cope with seeing themselves in an authentic light. Some people will insist we are someone we're not because they have to just to carry on.

If we want to be happy, we have to accept that we cannot control how other people see us. We can give the audition of a lifetime—and in nine out of ten theaters we would have just cinched the starring role—but in this one, at this moment, we're getting cast as the cow who doesn't matter. Or the side character who is only there to further the main character's growth, or the very wicked woman who is rotten to her core and dies jealous, brittle, and unloved by all in the audience.

That's okay. We don't need to be the star of every stage. We don't even need to be the good guy. It's okay if somewhere a group of people spend a night witnessing a story told from someone else's perspective, and they leave thinking we might be kinda trash. Every good story needs a villain, and it seems only right we get a chance to try on all the roles our stories have to offer. No one escapes life without at least one auditorium of humans who hate them enough to make passive-aggressive statements about them on the internet. The hard part is understanding that it's not personal, that it's often not about us at all.

I hope that we can learn to let one another carry on the way we need to. I don't mean, like, let a diagnosed narcissist gaslight the shit out of us for years because we're compassionate. I mean within the context of a few people who care for each other doing their best, I hope we can make room for the moments when we don't see eye to eye and we need to take a bow. We can decide to pass on the part offered to us and take a break from our loved ones' stages, or we can show up in the way they've decided they need us to if it's something we want to do. We can take to our own work and rewrite who we are over and over again. We can accept that sometimes people change and no longer fit the role that they used to.

Only we have the power to decide who we are. Someone else's perspective can feel unfair and even a little bit cruel, but it does not change the truth about us. Being misunderstood does not make us unimportant, unlikable, or evil. It is each of our jobs to be as honest as we can about the way we experience life, and we cannot dictate if others are capable of telling our truth. While feedback is helpful, and our companions can reflect something about ourselves back in a way we haven't seen, if we do the hard work to be a person we're proud of, we don't have to respond to being cast, inexplicably, as the cow. We can carry on telling our story, every night, to a packed house and a standing ovation. And we can hope the same for the many different theaters with many different shows being put on by the people we want the best for.

Flowers to the Hilltop

How many versions of me have I buried on a hilltop
in the sun somewhere?
I've lost count, to be honest,
but I bring flowers to their graves when I'm feeling kind.

I'm sorry to the people who knew me when my pain washed
    around my feet
and lapped at your ankles like an unexpected wave.
I'm sorry for the way I always walked unsteady—
for the hurt I spilled onto your white carpets.

But I hope you can forgive me,
or maybe, loan me grace?
I always seem to need it,
and I'm always short these days.

I hope that nature grows flowers that bring bees
where they lay.
They did the best they could with what they had.
We did the best we could with what we had.

And I know I haven't written my last eulogy,
but that's okay—

all my favorite people have dirt beneath their nails,
and freckles on their face.

heart surgeons, grizzly bears & the horrible, stubborn slowness of growth

I fucking hate a cliffhanger.

I like finality. I like it when the story has a beginning, a middle, and a nice, resounding end. I want my sentences to finish in definitive punctuation. Period.

When I was fourteen, I discovered *Grey's Anatomy*. Dr. Cristina Yang, top of her class at Stanford and ruthless competitor, fast-walked her way onto my screen and right into my heart. She knew the answer, she solved the problem, and she made choices fast with no hesitation. She wasn't just good—she was the best, and her world was black and white.

Her best friend and co-intern, Dr. Meredith Grey, couldn't have been more different. She was smart, but she wasted it. She was weak-willed and made mistakes because she wanted love more than she wanted to win. She did things that were shady, she loved the wrong people, and she routinely languished between a rock and a hard place she'd really set up herself. Meredith earned her name. Her world, and the way she saw right and wrong, were painted entirely in shades of gray.

I hated Meredith. I thought she was sloppy and messy and

lacked discipline. She spoke in run-on sentences, and even her passionate speeches were often riddled with ellipses you could practically reach out and pluck from the space in the stairwell where they hung between her and McDreamy.

I was pro-Cristina and anti-Meredith, and that was black and white to me. Most of my young life was characterized by severe, binary thinking. Things were right and things were wrong. People were good and people were bad. There was no such thing as a gray area.

My reliance on a hyper-defined worldview manifested in my life in more ways than being in the Cristina Yang fan club. It contributed heavily to my investment in Evangelical Christianity. When confronted with a hard topic, Christians don't usually say, "Huh, I don't know! I don't have an opinion on that—I guess, to each their own!" Their sentences end in very holy, very blessed periods and exclamation marks, and that was irresistible to me. I kept my life in strict control without any dalliances into deviancy. I didn't drink, smoke, date, or get anything below an A. When I got my first B+ in an accelerated math course, I couldn't get out of bed for three days.

Soon after beginning high school, it started to feel like controlling my own life was not enough. I was Cristina, and all my friends were acting like Merediths. So my friends, who had started sneaking out to meet long-haired skaters and slipping beers out of the fridge late at night, stopped talking to me about anything of importance. I was not a friend who would tenderly help untangle the strange feelings of excitement, guilt, shame, and hope of growing up and making reckless choices. Talking to me was more like confessing to your pastor you'd been finger-blasted[1] on your Bible-study leader's couch. My life was

---

1. Do people still say "finger-blasted?" Did they ever?

clean, focused, and good, and the pain I believed was coming
from their sloppy self-indulgence had an easy remedy. There
were simple choices in life—you could do the right thing, or you
could do the wrong thing—and it all came down on you. Their
behavior was wrong and I'd tell them so; they needed a little
tough love, and I was going to be top of my class at Stanford.

I couldn't understand when they started to cut me out of
their lives. I was just trying to help them, to keep them good.
Didn't they know what happened to people who ignored the
rules and chased after the wrong things? Those people suffered.
I was trying to *save* them from the path they were walking down
before they ended up with a *Go Ask Alice*–style journal that
chronicled their descent into self-destruction. In my home I'd
always learned that you have to be responsible for your choices
and what they bring you. You couldn't complain about the rabid
grizzly bear tearing up your couches when you'd invited it into
your house. No one ever met me in the messy middle and told
me that it was okay to screw up, and I was just *fine*. In my fourteen years I'd learned one thing: being held to an impossibly
high standard was the same thing as being loved. So I'd push
harder, and they'd pull back farther. I felt like I was on a desperate mission to keep my friends safe, and they probably felt like
they were in a high-speed chase, pursued by their youth group
leader, foaming at the mouth and burning rubber in a minivan.

My dedication to maintaining a black-and-white world cost
me in ways I couldn't fully understand, but I was *right*, goddamnit goshdarnit. I was being good. I wrote my story in clean
sentences that always ended in punctuation.

Then I grew up.

Life grabbed me by the nuggets and twisted, and that bitch
has an iron grip. I felt the sting of financial insecurity, of unrequited love, and of being so very tired you fall asleep with your

shoes still on. I was starting to realize that the world was not so black and white, and that people have to make a lot of choices they'd make differently if they had more support. I felt completely out to sea.

Confused and exhausted, I sought out comfort wherever I could find it. I came across my *Grey's Anatomy* box set, which I hadn't seen in years, and let out a deep sigh of relief. Who doesn't want to revisit an old friend when they feel lost? I was ready to reexperience the rush I felt when I was young and imagined traching someone in a restaurant while they choked.[2] Cristina would remind me what it takes to have my life together. She'd guide me back to my old self, tell me to kick my ass into gear and deal with it. I was certain, by the end of season one I'd be back in action, the head of cardio in the hospital of my life, wearing dark, flattering scrubs and rocking a truly unique scrub cap some heartsick intern would inevitably try to steal and hoard in their locker.

Barely an episode in the truth crashed into me hard enough to inspire a new mass trauma event storyline. I wasn't Cristina Yang anymore. I was *Meredith Fucking Grey*.

If fourteen-year-old me could have seen me then, she would have added my name to her list of pitiable women who needed to grow a backbone. Midtwenties me, though? I'd been beaten up and tossed around, and I actually, horrifyingly, *understood* Meredith.

She was just a girl with a broken heart doing her best.

And Cristina? She wasn't any different. She'd just buried

---

2. Traching is shorthand for performing a tracheotomy—in which you shove something like a straw into the windpipe to create airflow underneath whatever blockage is causing your patient not to breathe. Because of *Grey's*, I am irresponsibly sure that I could successfully trach someone with a hollowed out carrot or a BIC pen and a pocketknife.

her pain so deeply under the layers of success and control that she couldn't hear the same sick, wet hitch in her heartbeat. She couldn't hear her heart at all.

I rewatched episode after episode, and each one felt brand new. Going through so many hard things had given me a new perspective, and what I previously wrote off as weakness and failing, I saw now as the inevitable cost of being a person who wants to be okay. Meredith was trying, despite all of the abandonment and neglect and loss she had endured, to believe that life could still be good. Her messy, half-baked choices were proof of her stubborn, courageous hope. Cristina's decisiveness and finality were not a result of her superior self-control, but a symptom of her fear of not having the answers. The things I used to see as strength and moral sturdiness were just the thrashings of someone desperate to control what they could not, desperate to outsmart their aching, lonely heart. They had to learn that being right was not the same thing as being safe.

In the wake of my disillusioned journey to Seattle Grace, I needed to confront myself. It was clear that the black-and-white binary way I'd framed all of my choices and relationships was misguided and destructive, but I didn't know how else to understand the world. If I accepted that I didn't actually have the answers, I'd be left out to sea without a driftwood scrap to cling to. I could stomach being wrong, but I couldn't just float in limbo, untethered and drifting while life stayed difficult around me. I had to be rooted in *some* truth, or I was sure I'd be swept away. I couldn't handle being stuck in the in-between. Gray has never been my color.

So I didn't change with grace. I built a new framework in my head that had Right, Wrong, and Gray Area boxes, and I wanted to sort everything neatly away. I scrolled through my past choices like I was scrolling through an index, seeking everything that no longer felt secure and filing it into the "gray area, to be reevaluated" file. I sought a Yes and a No. You were wrong, now get right. I tried to force the comfort and confines of a binary to corral the shapeless nature of growth. I was desperate to leave behind the person I *was* and arrive immediately at the new, evolved version of me. My attempts were clunky and heavy, and I kept thinking I was done when I wasn't. It wasn't perfect, but I thought if I could control the chaos, I could work through the Gray box until every last homeless thought had been categorized and tucked away. I was rushing growth, frantically trying to pen the end of so many unfinished sentences.

Growth does not like to be rushed. I expected to cut into my body, find the tumor, and excise it with clean edges, but the tumor had tendrils growing into every corner. I couldn't get it out without cutting something vital. If I tried to remove one cancerous belief, it would destabilize another part of my life that I'd built upon it. The more I cut the more unsteady I felt, and the more unsure I felt about the world and my place in it. But I was impatient and ready to be off the operating table, out of the OR. I wanted to be healthy, recovering, and ready to move on with a new lease on life—without a hint of the worldview that had eaten away at me left behind to corrupt my heart. I wanted to be done changing.

But growth is a flowing, timeless thing, and I didn't know how to see that. You go to war against the grizzly in your living room with banging pots and an old hockey stick, edging her outside inch by inch until you slam the door and lock it. You think you have expelled the monster you once let into your home, so you decide which of your couch pillows are done for and which can be saved, and you get to work sewing up the gashes. Life moves on, and you feel changed after staring fuzzy death in the face and surviving, so you carry on living with your head held high. It is not until sometime later that you hear something suspicious coming from the guest room you never go into, and you open the door to find that the grizzly left a few cubs behind who have been neglected and hungry. Cubs that have been growing big and angry in the dark, and are now completely destroying your goose-feather duvet.

My cubs were hiding in the room with my relationships.

I was feeling pretty good about all the self-reflection I'd done and all the ways I'd challenged myself to see the world differently. If the old me had thought sex before marriage was wrong, the new me thought that it was for each person to decide, and the right thing to do was to let people choose for themselves. Period. I was so much less judgmental, less harsh, and easier to talk to. I'd reworked my understanding of life, and I believed passionately that there were many questions that had no right or wrong answer, only the space to be curious and kind. Many of my friendships were flourishing as I became a safer and safer place to bring pain and lay it down. There was a lot of proof that I'd powered right through the threat of limbo and successfully transformed. I was confident that this new me could quickly tie up any loose ends the old me had left behind.

When I ran into a place of friction with some old friends who'd known the old me, I knew I could fix it right away. Friction, I told myself, is just what happens when you've known each other for such a long time, and we could handle it. I asked to meet and talk through what was happening, but they asked for space. They wanted to just hit pause on the issue for a nameless period of time and leave me floating in the gray unknown. Before I even had a chance to stop myself, I was raging against the threat of being left without an answer, and I didn't let anyone "take space." I called, and texted, and I insisted if we could only talk about it then we could sort it out. I'd give it a day or two, then reach out again. Maybe a week, then reach out again. I couldn't let it go. It made me sick to my stomach to have one of my favorite stories with all my favorite characters trailing off into an unfinished sentence, when I knew I could sit down and finish it if they'd only do the right thing and be honest with me.

It didn't work. I pushed all the friends who just needed a minute to gather their thoughts much farther away. I'm sure it felt like I was poking a bruise, asking them where they got it, if they forgave me for it being there, and if it was feeling any better yet. After all, I was covered in bruises, and *I* carried on. Why couldn't they? Didn't they know it would heal either way, and I could help if they let me? For all my work to accept the gray areas, the obvious manifestation of my old black-and-white comfort zone into my refusal to give someone the space they needed was completely lost on me. If I had slowed down, taken a breath, and accepted the discomfort of the in-between, I might have heard the suspicious snuffling and grumbling coming from the other room before it became a full-blown roar. To this day I'm sure that some of my friendships have been left behind because it was easier to walk away than it was to fight off the grizzly that had surprised us both by tearing through my house and straight into theirs.

My guttural discomfort with the unknown and the unfinished made my world smaller than it should have been. I'm jealous of the people born with grayscale hearts. They are often the sort who lead with their emotion and instinct. They let the feelings wash over them, then they retreat with it all boiling up in their mind, and they turn down the heat before it boils over. They are the sort who take space. They are the sort who know that there's enough time to sift through it all.

I wasn't born that way, but I'm learning. I'm starting to be okay with the fact that life might be a series of short-story assignments. Ones that begin all passion and pressing ink into your best paper, then get left half written with an ending that never comes. We cannot arm-wrestle life into unfolding in tidy chapters. Sometimes we aren't even the author of the story we're invested in, and we're left wondering if the person with the power to choose what happens next will ever come back to us. There are cliffhangers and hard questions and plot lines that we might not get to finish—even the ones with the characters we loved the most. Stories with old friends we could have sworn we'd write about until we couldn't hold a pen might get put into a drawer and never get picked up again. Our only choice is to carry on living and breathing in the in-between, accepting that life is sometimes gray, and choosing stubborn, courageous hope.

I'm still no expert in letting go of things, but I'm trying. When I find another grizzly bear in my house to chase away, I take some time afterward to search through other rooms for the cubs she left behind. Sometimes they want to go be free immediately, and sometimes they need a little cuddle and some understanding before they can be pushed out of my heart and into the wild. I don't love having to pause my momentum to nurture a baby grizzly before it grows up and demands my attention, but I do my best to care for them and keep my furniture safe. If the story I'm writing comes to an abrupt, unfinished end, I leave it be and try to write something new with the hope that it might find me in the future. I do my best to lean on compassion while I'm not feeling very clearheaded, and I try to remind myself to embrace the discomfort of messy, muddled growth.

Sometimes I'm Cristina. Sometimes I'm Meredith. Sometimes I'm in the writers' room, trying to come up with something that will move the story forward and banging my head against the wall. But in the end, I can believe there's something beautiful about sentences that end in . . .

Could it be something like peace?

a messy bitch's guide to letting go

1. Whether or not you believe you *can* do something will often be the truth.
2. You are never too old or in too deep to change your life.
3. Even the people we love most in the world will not be with us forever.
4. Who you were when you were trying to survive does not need to haunt you. You are allowed to forgive yourself now that you know better.
5. Holding on to things when they do not want to stay will only bring you pain. Some things only stay when they feel comfortable. Your fear that they may leave you might be the very thing that makes them want to go.
6. Life does not happen the way you think it will when you are twenty years old.
7. You are more than what you have done or what you have not.
8. You will make people angry and uncomfortable when you grow. Grow anyway.
9. How people feel about you is none of your business.

Everyone can think whatever they want. You have your own thoughts to discover.

10. You are capable of very great things, and you do not need to wait until somebody else notices.

11. No one has to give you permission for your choices to be valid.

12. You might have to accept that no one will be at the finish line to cheer when you finish the race.

13. Some people who loved you once will not love you anymore.

14. The people who will love us in the way that we deserve need room in our lives to find us.

15. Healing makes things hurt a lot worse before it can make them better. You cannot abandon it halfway.

16. Some of the greatest things in your life may very well last the least amount of time.

17. Other people will have the things you want, the things you think you deserve. You can wish you had those things too, but you cannot harbor bad feelings for them because they have what you do not.

18. Security and safety are an illusion, there is no reason to try to hide from change.

19. It is very likely that fear will be your companion all your life. You must find a way to listen to its voice, but not follow its command.

20. You will always be subject to unfair critique. People want you small. Do not waste your time defending. They will critique. You will carry on.

21. Being alone is a very wonderful way to be when you have learned to enjoy your own company.

22. There will be time that you feel that you have wasted. It will make you sad. That's okay. You are still alive. You still have tomorrow.

what if no one remembers me?

There are certain friendships that are goddamn hard to lose. I might not have the right to say it, but I think they're harder to lose than romance. When you're building a relationship with a romantic partner, you build a trapdoor as you lay down the hardwood slabs. Those relationships are either going to end in forever or they're just going to end, and the odds aren't in your favor. You know from that first laugh and smile and touch it will probably end in someone's aching heart. So you slip a rug over the ridges on the floor, and sometimes in the dark when it's late and they're sleeping, you run your fingers over the place you might escape to if disaster blooms between you.

Friends, though? That's different. No trapdoors hidden in the blueprints. No emergency lever to pull.

You know that card at every party store that's a drawing of the backside of old women, fat and saggy and naked, with their feet dangling over a dock and their heads thrown back in laughter? They're laughing at Time and all the things it's given and taken, because after it all, they're still just giggling girls with their toes in the water—still together—after so much has happened.

When you meet a friend like that you feel it. You see the card of the wrinkly, saggy women and you think, "*That'll be us.*"

I'm a friendship person. I collect friends quickly, and surely, and for a long time I liked to brag, "I have more friends than anyone I know." I used to say that quite a bit.

Things are different now.

When I was young, I sought out other families to keep me safe and dry in the storm of my own home. It was messy, and it was vicious, and the waves could have drowned any one of us if we'd lost our footing. I couldn't rest, or play, or grow—I couldn't turn my back on the ocean.

So I found my footing in other little girls' houses. *Their* parents would give me cup-of-noodle soups and bologna and sourdough toast dripping in butter. *Their* parents never left me feeling confused about if I was a good person or if I was easy to love. I clung to my friends like the only scrap of driftwood still floating from a shipwreck, and I loved them fiercely. It felt like my life depended on it.

For some of us, our friends are the only thing that keep us tethered to what it means to feel loved and cared for. My very best friend for most of my life was the only person on planet Earth who had never wavered in her insistence that I was beautiful enough as I was. Imagine being a little girl surrounded by adults who told you to slim down and tighten up and earn your place in the cold, marble gallery of Womanhood. Then imagine your buddy, all buck teeth and bad haircut, saying for the five hundredth time, "They're crazy. You're the most beautiful person I know," before she passes you Cheese Nips.[1]

---

1. She was a Cheese Nip person, not a Cheez-It person—and I can forgive her for that.

She might as well have been passing me the last seat on the last *Titanic* lifeboat.

I've mentioned her before, but I want to take the time to really explain exactly what happened and exactly why it broke my heart. See, in our friendship, we gave the love we couldn't find in our families to each other. I would protect her when she was vulnerable. She would comfort me when my heart was scarring over another wound. We grew up like that—two kids who felt lost in the woods fashioning spears out of sticks and vines and walking back to back, knowing we'd take turns keeping watch during the night.

All the way into adulthood, it had never stopped feeling like we were kids in the dark woods. It had never stopped feeling like we might die if the other one left. At least, it hadn't stopped for me.

The end had been coming for a while before it finally caught up with us. There was a cascading series of misunderstandings and saying things we couldn't ever really take back. One of us would forgive while the other couldn't, and then we'd trade places. When we would see each other, I always had the same sensation of being too high up in cold mountains. The air was thin and tinny, and my lungs never felt full. We might laugh, and we might eat and drink, but underneath it all the ice was splintering. So we talked over the cracking sound and reached for each other's hands, but our eyes pinned the truth between us: *it was too late.* Our steps, no matter how lighthearted we tried to be, were falling too heavy for a foundation already falling apart.

You know those movies where someone is dying, and someone else is holding their face in their lap? The not-dying person is saying ridiculous things like, "You're gonna be fine. We'll go to Aruba. We'll drink piña coladas, and we'll dance all night, and we'll sleep in while the waves crash outside!" And the not-dying person is laughing softly while they cry, while the dying person is smiling weakly with unfocused, glassy eyes, and you can start to see the stars reflecting in the slick, dark pool growing beneath them both.

I cannot describe to you the sadness of nursing your dearest friendship to death. I cannot describe to you how brutally your heart is torn in two as you babble on about Aruba, and the wicked way you'll laugh when you're old women, with the starlit pools beneath you.

I wouldn't wish that pain on anyone at all. I'm sorry if you know it, too.

After a long few years of tending to what felt like a bird with a too-badly broken wing, the bonds of my friendship with my closest friend fell apart. We'd been patching holes with duct tape and sheer force of will, but we couldn't patch fast enough, and the water was at our necks. In the end, she couldn't forgive me for what she believed I'd done, and I couldn't confess to an intention I'd never had. So we had the final talk. We said, "I'm sorry it had to come to this," and, "I wish it wasn't this way," and, "I'll always love you," and, "I'm so grateful to you—for it all." Finally, we accepted that some wings cannot be healed. We buried that precious thing that was so tired in the garden. We said the word *goodbye*.

In medieval times, one of the many creative ways white people liked to kill each other was called pressing.[2] They'd lay heavy thing after heavy thing on someone's chest, slowly squeezing the air out of the lungs and exhausting the muscles trying to usher it back in. Gradually, under all that weight, the person suffocated.

---

2. White people really have always just been brutal and weird about killing people—we needed to get a medieval grip, my dudes.

Every letter in the word *goodbye* weighs a ton. I'm sure of it. I felt like I couldn't breathe.

Once, when I was speaking with my dad on the anniversary of his brother's death, he said that one of the biggest reasons he misses his brother wasn't one he had expected. He missed his brother because his brother's memory was so good. My dad's memory has always been shit. His brother used to visit at Christmas, and once a year I'd watch the original Donalson family in the living room they'd gathered in for fifty years, telling stories about the adventures they'd taken when they were all so young. I don't hear many stories about when they were all so young anymore.

It's just my dad and his mom now. She's old.[3] So between the laughing and dad jokes and random life updates that usually compose our phone calls, my dad said to me, "Once Nana goes, that's it. All those memories from our family will be gone. I don't remember any of them. It will be like our history is wiped away. It will be like it never happened." This made me want to immediately start chronicling the family history, imagining long talks with Nana over iced tea on the porch. But then I remembered that the woman and her son (and her granddaughter) all have rampant ADHD and cannot focus on anything longer than three minutes. Nana especially. Playing board games with Nana ends in her making up her own rules and usually wearing a game piece on her head like a little hat. It has always been this way.

The thing about losing someone who was there for all your most important and hardest moments is that you lose your history too.

My friend was my chosen family. She was the one who would comfort me after a scary moment with my parents, making sure I could breathe through it. Her house was the

---

3. She won't mind me saying this, as she reminds me every time I call.

place I'd get suddenly sent to when the air got crackly and electric in mine. We'd be watching *SpongeBob* in her living room while my parents were yelling the way you can't yell in front of kids back at my house.

And while my parents did their best, there were a lot of things that happened that they didn't want to remember. Or maybe they really didn't remember them, the way your mind lets memories that hurt too much loose and never calls them back. When I'd bring them up I got told, "God, you love to make things up, Devrie. That never happened."[4]

My friend remembered, though, and it kept me sane. Despite the gaslighting of my family, she had been there, had seen it and heard it, and she would tell me I wasn't crazy. She would tell me I was good. She was the only other person on Earth I could count on to believe that the things that had shaped my life had been real at all.

"When she's gone, that's it. My family history will be wiped away. It will be like it never happened."

When that friendship died, so did my chances of having anyone believe me about such important things. I'd spent so much of my life desperately wanting to be *believed*. I felt like I was alone in a dark wood full of hungry, floating eyes, and it made me desperate and afraid. Without her, suddenly I was the only one left who remembered. I had to ask myself: *Can that be enough?*

It's one thing to talk about the joys of being alone in the context of adventure and self-care and face masks and girl power. It's another to talk about being alone in the context of being the only person on the planet who really knows who you are.

---

4. God, it must be hard to be a parent. Especially when you are only a kid yourself.

We all want the feeling of being known. We crave a witness to our story. It's the greatest gift we can offer another—just the feeling of being seen. When we can't come alongside someone on their path, we can acknowledge that it's real. I can't sink into the depths of grief with the one who's lost their mother, and I can't elevate to the height of joy of one marrying their dream partner, but I can witness it. I can say, "I see you, right there on that spot on the hill you're climbing, and I know where you are. I cannot join you, but I can see you." Loneliness is more about wanting to be noticed than it is about wanting to have company.

Isn't that the truth about losses? All those moments and conversations and choices that became the building blocks of your life, the material you've used to create who you are, suddenly feel less real. Who will remember you now? Who will know your story?

And isn't that the truth about love? It's the little moments where you build together. Be it friend or family or lover—we weave the tapestry of who we are out of the long-distance phone calls, the late-night TV giggles, pointless drives, skinny-dipping, burned dinners, and the petty fights. We give and we take and we loan each other what we can as we lay our foundations, polish the floors, and put up the drywall of our time on Earth. We show up to paint walls. We eat dinner off of moving boxes. Love is a pair of paint-covered overalls with patches on the knees.

I can't tell you that I'm an expert on how to move on from grief. It surprises me all the time. Grief, as far as I understand, is an ever-changing, ever-present companion from the moment it fills the space left in your heart by someone you once built a place for.

I can tell you, though, that being your own history keeper is enough. You don't need to have somebody else to validate that you are who you are for a reason. If there's one thing I've learned, it's that none of us, no matter how surefooted we are in our lives, can count on someone else to never leave. People *leave*. It's in our nature. Whether it's our choice or it's death or it's the way change takes its toll, no one gets to choose to stay forever. The only person we can always be there for is ourselves.

So, believe yourself. Love yourself. Root for yourself. Hold your own memories dear and precious. Reach backward into time and be ready to take the hurting kid into your arms. I know "Inner Child Stuff" has been a real buzzy topic on the internet, but it really does help. I've met my younger self in a lot of echoing rooms, and I have never left. We're in it together these days, she and I. I keep her memories safe. She didn't have many safe adults back then, and nobody believed her. She has me now, and I do.

Once I accepted the loss of my history folded within the loss of my friendship, the panicked part of my heart that reacted like it was life or death got quiet. I wasn't angry or vicious or panicked anymore. I wasn't desperate to survive. I was just sad. I am just sad these days.

It has already gotten better, and I'm sure that the sting will continue to soften with time. But for now, I'm okay with the quick knife-slip of missing her, because it's not about my survival anymore. It's about her, and the ways we laughed, and the things we saw and did and discovered. It's about all the complicated ways we helped each other grow up. It's about the place in my chest that always aches when it rains.

I'm thankful to have loved someone that much without ever building a trapdoor into the floorboards. It all came down around us, we couldn't get out unscathed, but I don't think either one of us would have done it differently. We loved and built and broke, and in many ways, it made us who we are. I'm proud of who I am. I'm proud of who she is too.

But I did learn a lesson.

I'll never turn another person into the keeper of my life and my history. I'll never hand someone the bits of me that need the most love and care, and hope that they can commit to carrying them always. I'll carry those things myself, even if my arms are sore and my hands are tender.

I'll *share* a gorgeous life with so many people yet to come, though—I know it. What's that phrase I love? Something like, "There are so many more people who are going to love you. You haven't even met them yet." I believe that's true for all of us. There will always be another bottle to open in my home and my heart for the person who got there late and needs a drink.

But no matter how late they are arriving, I'll never mourn my empty rooms again. I'm building this house with the love I know I can't lose. My history is written on its walls in broad strokes I can run my fingers over—some tragic, some triumphant—and all of them mine. This house, this *life*, is a monument to the deepest friendship of all. No trapdoor required.

This healing business is really just:
- Crying yourself to sleep for a year,
- And having no one to call when your grandfather dies,
- And answering every text with: "Yes, I promise, I am totally fine."

It's one long, dark, and very lonely night.
You can only try to stay warm and survive it.

The secret, I have found, is giving up on forcing the sun to rise,

Because the lesson is this:
- The sun doesn't come when it's called,
- The sun only comes when it's ready.

outer space, felonies & the delicate magic of zooming out

I'm not allowed to look at space for too long.

I get yelled at. Sometimes when my brother calls, he'll hear a telltale weird undertone in the way I'm talking and he'll know it's gone too far. He's the most gentle person I know, but he doesn't hesitate to bark, "Have you been lookin' at space again? Stop lookin' at space!"

Let me explain.

It usually starts when I get so overwhelmed by all the things I'm responsible for that I freeze. I'm fine until I'm not, and then I'm *super* not.

The universe has often seen fit to hand me many plates—way too many plates—and I had no option but to keep the plates spinning. I had to eat, and I had to have healthcare, and I had to pay my student loans, so I couldn't just pull up to the coast and watch the sun go down, now could I? Life demands from us. It often demands too much, but you can't just die under a bridge, so you find a way to soldier through it. Even if it feels like you're barely even there.

There have also been times in which my life was

uncharacteristically calm, and I couldn't stand the quiet, so I sought out the noise myself.

I'd like to tell you that if I had the money to live a simple life off the coast of Italy, wearing silk scarves in my hair and eating summer tomatoes right off the vine, I would. I'd like to think that's true. To think that the beauty of a slow life—free of the pressure to work or perform or outwit capitalism—would be enough for me.

But challenge is a drug, and I'm a junkie. I don't know how much money it would take to pull me away from the lure of filling my life with higher and higher peaks to climb. I'm always outrunning something, or chasing something, and I don't rest very well either way. I thrive under pressure, and I love the feeling of getting a gold star. If I'm not pushing my brain to try new and more challenging things, I feel like it's just a little raisin in the making—crisping up in the sun. If I'm not moving, something wicked is coming my way, and I'll also probably die of atrophy.

Whether universe-given or self-destructively created, the scales tip too far, and I get overwhelmed. Overwhelmed enough to freeze while the responsibilities and promises I made start gathering like a heavy, pregnant storm cloud right over my head. No matter how I try, I can't reach into it and pull down something solid to work on. It's just foreboding mist, no structure or body, gathering and getting darker. Eventually, after enough threatening, it storms, and I never have an umbrella. There's my sorry ass, caught in the rain that I brought on myself—not a piña colada in sight.

Desperate, overwhelmed, and soaked to the bone *without* a tropical beverage and nowhere else to go, I turn to look at space.

You see, space is a thing with no container. What else can you say has no beginning and no end? Time? I can't *look at* time, unless you count looking at the fine lines that crinkle my face, which showed up with so much unexpected gusto when I turned thirty they were practically naked and twerking on a wrecking ball.

When you look up at the night sky, you're looking at something with *no ending*. It's a vastness humans can't even wrap their minds around. It's dotted with planets and galaxies, burning stars and dying stars, and black holes that start from nothing and lead to nowhere.[1] That's all swirling around like a giant eff-the-rules tornado, and I'm down here making myself sick over my Gmail inbox? My puny, planetless *inbox?!*

I won't have it. I look up and remember I'm just stardust, baby.

It helps to put things into the perspective of me versus the universe. There's an instant sense of relief. A weight gets lifted off my shoulders when I realize that in the context of the endlessness of space, me being behind on answering emails or unsure of what to post on the internet is really, really a waste of time. The *issue* is that once I start to think about how very gloriously insignificant we are, and *just* how pointless it is to worry about an inbox, things can get a little funky.

I mean, if my inbox doesn't matter at all, does . . . my *life?* Too much stargazing, and I start to get a little too far into the "*nothing matters lolz*" camp. I start reposting nihilist memes. I sing "Don't Worry, Be Happy," stop brushing my hair, and start craving piña coladas at noon. Right about the time I'm toying with becoming a career criminal, I'll get a phone call from my brother, who will tell me about a bird he saw eating an ice cream cone in the Costco parking lot. He'll sense a little

---

1. I have no idea about the actual mechanics of black holes, and to be honest, I don't care to know. I want to carry on in my ignorance and let the sort of people with NASA stickers on their cars shake their heads at me. I'm very comfortable with that.

too much lime in da' coconut and yell at me, lovingly, to peel my eyes from the sky and get my shit together.

I am a gal in search of balance. I have yet to perfectly crack the code on how to live a life with purpose and intention without being far too attached to the outcome, but I do have one little trick I rely on when I'm caught in the middle, frozen by overwhelming choice and life, I'd love to share with you.

When I find myself in a moment of choice, at a crossroads, or even cowering under the impending doom of the cloud of overwhelm, I try to zoom out. I zoom out and look at myself like I'm watching a movie or reading a book, watching the main character and waiting to see what she'll do next. I imagine that I'm sharing this book with a friend, or I'm telling this story in a year or two, and I ask, "What needs to happen next for this to be a story I'm proud to tell?"

I think of the person I want to be and what she might do— get a really good idea of what would make an excellent story with a character I'd be excited to root for—then I zoom back in to myself. And even if I'm so overwhelmed I can't get out of bed, even if I've been looking at space for way too long and am on Do Not Disturb mode while I research bank heists, I can see what I have to do to be proud of who I am. Then I do my best to make the choice that spins my life into a story I'm proud to tell.

Zooming out has helped me in many moments so far. It's particularly helpful when I'm worn so thin that I want to react instantly to feeling hurt. *What would someone I'd look up to say? Would they press Send on the text I just spent ten minutes typing out like I wanted to punish my tiny keyboard for existing? Probably not, buddy. Probably not.*

It's also been a crucial tool when I'm overwhelmed by a big choice. I know I'm not the only one who's been confronted by a situation that feels like it has no solution—one where the stakes are high and what you choose to do next will change everything. When I find myself there, I zoom out. Instead of driving myself crazy, analyzing every single molecule of the thing and trying to play out the ending to a conclusion that feels certain, I decide to be certain of *myself* instead. What choice would someone I root for make? If she's wrong, is she wrong for the right reasons?

I can't tell you I remember the old zoom-out trick all the time. I don't always have the presence of mind, or the strength of spirit, or the ability to think beyond the angry clouds above. Even when I'm feeling okay, my looking up sometimes leaves me wondering what crimes I should commit now that nothing matters at all.[2]

But when it does work—when I hit that sweet spot of perspective—it's wonderful, because I know I did my best. When the certainty that we're making the right choice is impossible, we can be certain of ourselves instead. I know I took a beat, and I weighed the options, and I made the best choice with what I had available. Maybe I still ended up breaking a plate, or disappointing the ghosts of my overachieving grandfathers, but I could meet them in the great beyond with my head held high. I could still say that everything I did, I did to become the best version of myself and to do the most good that I could.

We're all just little specks of stardust, swirling through space for a time so short anything older and bigger wouldn't even notice we were here. We love and we dance and make art out of dry macaroni. We teach each other how to count and how to read. We have favorite animals, and favorite stories, and favorite colors to wear around. We plant flowers and we wait all

---

2. For the record, I do not commit crimes. However, I've always wanted to see something very big burn down. *Allegedly.*

year for them to come back, just so we can wonder at the way the universe collided into the gentle curve of a perfectly white tulip. We're just barely there bits of celestial magic. We shouldn't be losing sleep over our inboxes.

Every day I'm better at zooming out, becoming a person I root for, and stargazing normally without feeling inspired to become a felon. I trust myself to do my best, and I don't feel so overwhelmed that I hear the heavens beckoning me to a life of crime. But just to be safe? I'll go to my grave without ever seeing *Interstellar*.

Unremarkable

I worked really hard,
for a really long time,
to be Undeniably
Unforgettably
Remarkable.

To earn the love I'd been denied.

But a lot of time has passed
since anyone expected greatness out of me.

"She used to be a real go-getter."

Now I rest my hands in my lap,
and I can almost recall the way they looked when I was
    younger,
and I think

An unremarkable life would suit me just fine.

who wants to share their testimony? who wants to face who they've been?

If you've ever spent any time in the American Evangelical Christian church, you've probably heard a hundred times, "Who wants to share their testimony?"

Sharing a testimony happens when someone gets up and tells how they "came to Jesus" or "found Jesus" or "found God," with the goal of wowing the crowd with a story that exhibits God's redeeming powers. People should be in tears, thinking, "If God can save a sinner like *them?* No one is out of reach!" It's meant to reinvigorate the part of you that longs to share the gospel. If a testimony is powerful enough, the congregation should leave knowing that the only thing stopping their drug-addict neighbor from getting sober and becoming a warrior for Christ is their own cowardice and doubt. Jesus can reach anyone, he just needs *you* to arrange a meet-cute so he can get to razzlin' and dazzlin'. In other words, you better start scheming a way to bring up J-Money with Ganja Gary from two doors down, or you're the one condemning him to an eternity of smokin' the Devil's lettuce with Hot Lucy himself.

Sharing testimonies is an art underscored with competition

and hierarchy.[1] You want to have the dirtiest, darkest past in the room so you can amaze the crowd with your squeaky-clean soul after the car-wash experience of God's grace. Sharing that you were a Sunday-school kid who never wavered or went prodigal son on anyone's ass doesn't get you invited to share your testimony on Sunday in front of the big church. That story is boring. It doesn't have impact or a shiny place for God to show off. Where's the hook?

I was a hookless Sunday-school kid. I didn't have a flashy past riddled with sex, drugs, and rock and roll. I was a born rule follower, and I was as boring as a Sunday sermon on the importance of tithing. Sometimes when I was asked to share, I'd try to weave a manufactured moment of doubt into my testimony, like, "*Why* would God create *cancer*?" But everyone knew the truth. I had been born into a Christian family, I had always been a Christian, and I'd never questioned it once.

I'd never questioned it, because Christianity was safe. It was a place where there was structure and a hard-and-fast set of rules I could use to conquer my greatest fears. Under the roof of the Christian church, I was good enough, and as long as I did what I was told, I would not be left behind. Even death couldn't separate me from the things I was terrified to lose. I could measure myself against my peers who *were* dabbling in sex or drugs or rock 'n' roll and know that I was heading to a golden-streeted eternity to skip Dorothy-style all through the Jesus party while they were risking eternity as Satan's favorite chew toy. In the world laid out for me by Christianity, if I lived my life the way Jesus wanted me to, I would be safe and accepted, so I never wavered in my faith, and my testimony stayed boring.

Now, the story of how I *abandoned* God? That one's much more exciting.

---

1. No one would admit it unless they're a bad girl like me.

It started in college, but this isn't a Spring Break Sinning Spree kind of tale. My university had the second-largest college-aged Christian organization out of all public schools in the country and offered a more robust Christian education than many of the private Christian schools had available.[2] From the moment I stepped foot onto that campus, I knew exactly where I belonged. I didn't start partying. I had no boyfriends or hookups during messy nights while I tested the limits of growing up. I didn't even drink until midnight on my twenty-first birthday, and after my single weak-sauce cocktail I marked the level on my new bottle of sweet tea vodka so my roommates couldn't make me an accomplice to their sin.[3] I rejected the opportunity to try anything scary and new because I already knew the ultimate truth, and I dedicated my entire college experience to furthering the word of God.

I had a very parochial worldview then. I had come from a conservative town, lived all of my life in church, and spent far too many school field trips at the Ronald Reagan Library learning about the Iron Man–level genius of trickle-down economics. I didn't believe in feminism, I didn't believe that racism was really still a thing, and I didn't believe in gay rights. I was a Bible-thumping, close-minded product of the first eighteen years of my life.

As I planned my future, I knew that you had to show some interest in or support of "diversity" if you wanted to find work in the competitive field of clinical psychology. My plan was to be a Christian therapist for teens who had gone through something

---

2. I think all young people, especially young Christian people, should go to schools where students are allowed to think and explore without the threat of expulsion for violating religious rules.

3. Dear College Roommates, I'd like to take this moment to formally say, I'm sorry for going full Mother Superior. I'm surprised no one referred to our house as the Nunnery. I owe you a bottle of sweet tea vodka.

like I had—a confusing experience with parents and addiction and mental health—and I knew I wouldn't need any sort of Liberal Girl badge in order to land that gig. But I would need to go to grad school, and grad school demanded some level of study of diverse people's lived experiences. I begrudgingly searched the course catalog for a handful of classes I could take as electives to strengthen my résumé and settled on Women's and Gender Studies 101.

I was not excited. My Christian friends and I rolled our eyes at the ridiculous world we were living in, bemoaning the fact that we had to pretend to be a part of some liberal agenda to even get a job in this country. I went to my first class like I was dressed in armor, already primed to write off anything I heard as absolute nonsense and to valiantly defend the teachings of God.

Initially, I did just that. I only listened to what the professor was saying to find opportunities to dismiss her arguments as the spicy lies of Ole Hot Pants downstairs. Every new day that I left class without feeling man-hatey and pentagrammy, I raised my glass to the Holy Spirit and toasted to his protection against the evils of feminism.

But something deep in my soul was stirring. I really did, underneath it all, want to do the most good I could for the world, and after a lifetime spent submerged in religion, I truly believed the God of the American Evangelical Church was *the* God of the world. I thought that in order to avoid suffering someone had to know Jesus, and the only way to save people from pain was to make sure they were a Christian. In my world, my efforts to spread and maintain the power of Christianity were for everyone's greatest good, not just mine. I was trying to do the right thing.

People in the Christian church are controlled with fear, even though most of them don't realize it. We are afraid of kicking the tires of our Jesus Mobile because the cost is the potential loss of the social and community support humans need to thrive. Losing both the safety of numbers *and* the promise of divine intervention between you and mortality is a very high price to pay for satiating curiosity or indulging in too-critical thought. Being cast out from your village can be a death sentence, and I didn't see any reason to risk it. I wasn't willing to wander the desert alone without untouchable proof that my religion wasn't what it said it was, and I didn't think that proof existed.

Until Women's and Gender Studies 101.

The devout among us weren't flocking to the feminist courses, so I found myself alone in my beliefs. During one class session a defiant boy who didn't register in time to get any other elective raised his hand and suggested, quite confidently, that according to evolution and whatnot, women were biologically weaker and meant to be subservient to men. He insisted that claiming women were equal to men, in any regard, was to violate the laws of nature. The other students and the professor immediately shut him down in a swift tide of righteous, educated anger, but I was quiet.

I turned what the woman-hating boy had said over and over in my head, trying to place where I'd heard it before. It was such a horrible thing to say, and so clearly at odds with how I felt about myself and my place in the world, but it felt so familiar. Suddenly, it hit me, like a revelation.

Kick the evolution bit, add a pinch of Adam and Eve with a rib in the garden, and you've got more or less the same recipe the future Tech Bro was cookin' up but with a Bible-flavored twist. How many sermons had I sat through talking about the ways that wives need to serve their husbands? Sure, they always came with some spin about husbands and wives representing equal parts of God, but they ended the same: Christian women, if your man is talking, shut the hell up. Even the most liberal Christians I knew wouldn't say "women can do anything that men can, and do not need to submit to their husbands in any regard because they are equally human and powerful" out loud. I realized for the first time how truly monstrous that sounded. Who would believe that I was meant to be subservient to someone like the asshole misogynist who couldn't even grow a mustache sitting next to me? And why wasn't everyone calling bullshit on the many pastors who loved to speak about their equal-but-submissive wives?

It was the crack in the windshield that started it all, and I became consumed with the pursuit of truth. I signed up for religious-studies courses and external Christian courses on missionary work and the word of God. I studied obsessively, hunting down the origin of things, their claims to divinity, and if you could prove that they were true, or if maybe . . . just maybe, if you could prove that they weren't. I had one foot in the village where everyone I knew and loved lived, and one foot in the world that seemed to think I was just as valuable as my brothers, but in which I would be alone.

The more I dug into Christianity from a historical and scholarly perspective, the more things started to fall apart. Without the mysticism of God obscuring everything that didn't quite make sense with some vague notion of Faith over Everything, the missing pieces were glaring and undeniable. I learned about the start of Christianity, from its very origins all the way up to modern interpretations, and the way the passages in the Bible were chosen by a group of men to reinforce a narrative they were invested in. I learned how it had been reconstructed over and over at different points in history to better inflict the power of the Christian rulers on the people they were subjugating, despite Christianity's claim to be unchanging. I thought about

how often God's will was used to justify global atrocities, despite
there being zero biblical evidence for God wanting anything to
do with what was being done. I learned that the things I'd been
told were the timeless opinions of God had only been ideas for
about fifty years, born of men who wanted to win elections
and get paid by politicians. In short, I learned that my religion
and everything I had chosen to do with my life was built on a
shallow, hole-riddled book built of smoke and mirrors, and in-
terpreted by powerful men to control the world and all of those
in it. It was not divinely breathed. The Bible and what we know
as Christianity in white America were man-made tools that had
very little to do with the will of any god, used to justify hurting
so many people for such a long time.

In the light of what I'd learned, I could not go on like nothing had changed. I believed that we'd all been misled, and that
learning about the ways humans had manipulated the true will
of God would inspire immediate change in pursuit of justice
and equity. When I tried to bring up the role of the church
in global inequality and the way we should feel responsible to
change, I was socially punished. Slowly and surely, people began
to treat me with less respect, make less eye contact, and sit farther and farther away. The male leaders who were my peers told
their girlfriends not to spend time with me. The pastors didn't
think that addressing inequality between men and women was
the church's responsibility. The more I pushed, the more I was
rejected. I felt a rising sense of panic in my chest. I was being
banished from my village, one day at a time.

I was having a very different experience in my WGS classes
and with the people I'd met there.

By the time I was ready to graduate, I had taken enough
WGS classes to earn myself a place in the honor society and a
WGS minor. One of our professors invited the honors students

to her home for an end-of-the-year celebration, and I went a bit timidly. I didn't know what to expect, and I was still trying to figure out what I did and didn't believe. My entire life was about Christianity, but it was clear I wasn't welcome if I kept insisting there were things we'd gotten wrong. I wasn't welcome if I couldn't accept that all of "God's" cruelty was really some sort of kindness human minds could never understand. And in a room full of the very people who had suffered so much of God's kindness, I felt like an outsider with a lot to atone for.

After a bit of mingling, we were asked to sit in a circle on the living room floor, just like the thousands of Bible studies and small groups I'd been to before. The professor cleared her throat and said, "I thought it might be nice if we went around the circle and shared the story of how we each became a feminist."

My heart flipped. We were sharing testimonies.

They began, one by one, talking about their journey toward believing in the inherent personhood and equal rights of all. Some were born into feminist households with feminist mothers who taught them to fight for their rights from the time they were toddling. Some had come to it when they realized at a young age that boys and girls were treated differently on the playground. Some had had a nasty boyfriend who sent them on a journey of self-empowerment. Some had realized they were a lesbian and had come to find their family. Then it was my turn.

I took a shaky breath and told them the truth. I was born into a family that believed in God and the teachings of the Christian church. I said that I'd come to their community cold, judgmental, and defensive, and that I'd been prepared to argue with them about their fundamental rights. But the more time I spent in their company, the more I learned how to shut down my programming and actually listen, because our classes were not a place of fear and threat, but of fierce belief and genuine love. I shared that I'd brought what I'd learned with them to the organization that had caused them so much pain, and that I'd been rejected for insisting we needed to ask ourselves hard questions.

Then I told them that they were the kindest, smartest, bravest group of people I'd met, and that they practiced the love that my church so loudly preached. I said I was so sorry for what we had brought to them and the ways they'd been targeted by the group I was a part of. I told them I was a baby feminist, and that I didn't know how to carry on with my dissonant identities, but I knew that it seemed like what I'd been taught about the world was a lie and that they deserved so much better. I asked for their forgiveness, and I thanked them for welcoming me.

It was disorienting to share my testimony of *leaving God behind* in order to find a true, redeeming love in a room full of people who were their own passionate, radical believers. I braced for the impact of their disgust and rejection. I wouldn't blame them if they chased me out the door with torches and pitchforks after what I'd just confessed. I was the reason they had been through so much unfair and unjust pain. Who would accept someone who had sinned so brutally against them?

When a hand reached out and lightly touched my shoulder, my entire body went still. I squeezed my eyes shut, waiting for them to ask me to leave, but a quiet voice simply said, "Thank you. Thank you for being here and for sharing that with us. The fact that you were so far gone but you found the courage to change gives me a lot of hope."

I didn't deserve their forgiveness, but they gave it freely without any strings attached. Even though they knew I wasn't one of them, they never made me feel like I didn't belong. They welcomed me into their sacred spaces and into their lives. The queer, feminist people I'd been raised to fear as the enemy sat with me, a dirty, low-down sinner, in the walls of their holy church, and they offered me rest. Their guiding light was not Jesus or the promise of eternal security in the face of the unknown, but rather the stubborn belief that everyone, no matter who you are or where you have been, deserves to be loved and to be free.

They reminded me more of the character of Jesus of Nazareth than a single one of the Christians I had spent my life beside. As I sat within the sanctuary of their friendship, I had never felt closer to the divine. But God, according to everyone who knew him, was very, very far away from us.

The foundation of my life and the reasoning behind every one of my great sacrifices was beginning to crumble beneath me, but I scrambled to keep it together. It was the reason I had left so many things untouched, why my life had been one of such rigidity, why I hadn't done any of the things my peers were doing and kept my world so small. To accept that it was all for nothing, even though I had every reason to do so, felt impossible.

I graduated and moved home with a heart full of questions and tension, but I just wasn't ready to give up Christianity altogether. I still believed in God and the teachings of Jesus. It was the *Christians* and their hypocrisy that I couldn't get behind. Those weren't the same thing, surely, humans and God. Human error. Misinterpretation. I could be a feminist who believed in human rights for everybody *and* be a follower of Jesus. There was room in the Kingdom of God for me. There had to be.

When my old youth pastor reached out to me and asked if I'd like to be the head of youth ministries at my church, I was ecstatic. I had a chance to help young people and to teach the word of God in a way that honored us all, not one that taught some as lesser and some as more. I didn't have the answers to everything, and I still had some beliefs I'd punch myself in the face for today, but I was trying. I wouldn't have to abandon everything I'd ever known or leave the church—my *home*. I could still do *good*.

I'd barely been in the office a week before I was confronted for sullying the word of God. I was admonished for having dyed hair (by a woman with very dyed hair) because I was modeling vanity to the girls. I was told that to say being gay or bisexual was anything but a class-A sin was a fireable offense. I was asked to speak to the girls about modesty, but only to the girls, because their summer clothes were causing the boys to stumble. I got so angry, and then so tired, and as I looked into the eyes of the kids who were trying so hard to understand their place in the world, I knew I was letting them down by participating in a place that insisted a made-up story be the only one told. I thought about how many people who had trusted me with something as precious as their worldview I had unintentionally led astray, and I realized how much harm I must have caused throughout my life. I didn't know how much longer I could find ways to justify sticking with Christianity and the person I chose to be there. I was starting to realize that good people who try to do good things couldn't know what I knew and believe what I believed.

In the midst of my crisis of faith, the Supreme Court passed Marriage Equality. I sobbed happy tears, thinking of the beautiful friends who woke up that day finally free to love, and I went to social media to take part in the celebrations.

Do you know what I saw instead?

Sickening, rotten outcry. Almost every post I saw from a Christian friend was some horrible, uneducated, and cruel rant about how God was mourning. How we were losing some invisible battle. About how we all should be wailing and fighting against the rising tide of Satan's hold.

Queer people just wanted to get fucking married.

I knew then, despite how much it was going to hurt, that those people were not my people, and their god was not my god.

As I distanced myself from the church, it became clear very quickly—anyone who'd cared about me either needed to win me back or reject me completely. It was not acceptable to embrace me for who I was becoming. They needed to fall in line and let me go or drag me home, or they'd be wandering the desert too. In the blink of an eye, I'd gone from feeling safe and secure amongst my forever friends to spending days and nights feeling entirely, desperately alone.

So there it was. One community who had suffered at my hand welcomed me to their table and offered me a place to sleep. One who I had given everything to, who preached an endless, ageless love, started ushering me into the cold the instant I suggested that perhaps we could be more loving. I'd been told that queer people and feminist women were the enemies and that I should react to them with fear and defensiveness. In reality, they were the exact opposite of what had been described, and the true enemy was the thing I thought would be my salvation. It is often the case in institutions that rely on fear and control that the most demonized outsiders are the very ones who could disprove and destabilize everything if they were truly understood.

The thing about big, life-shaping beliefs is giving them up hurts like letting go will kill you. Every single thing inside you will rage against it because accepting you made a lot of choices that were wrong and hurtful costs too much. It throws everything out of balance. Our bodies and minds strive for balance always.

Some beliefs are so hard to challenge because they promise protection from all the things we are most afraid of. Being alone, life and pain being pointless, feeling out of control, being vulnerable to more powerful people, and even death are swept away in the comfort of a worldview like Christianity. In return for security, they only ask for your unwavering servitude to the cause and unquestionable faith. There is no room for doubt or nuance, because love and control in places like that are the same exact thing.

That's why it took me so long to leave the church despite so much compounding evidence that I should. To change the entire belief system which we have used to build our life is to become radically and deeply unstable. Learning that you are not the person you believed yourself to be can be so disastrous to our psyches that we cannot face it when it first comes to us as truth. Starting over feels like an illness when we're just about to leap, and our systems fight illness without waiting for our permission. We often aren't aware of what's happening inside of us until the battle against acceptance has been waging for some time.

When I think of my own story, I can understand why there are so many folks who refuse to listen to anything new or contrary to what they have decided is true. Sometimes the people we love cannot accept what is right in front of them, because the reckoning is too painful. If they are *wrong*, then they have likely caused harm, but they aren't a bad person. They are good, and good people don't hurt others, so that they are wrong and responsible for the pain of others simply cannot be true. If they are wrong, the things they are most afraid of will be untamed again, and that could ruin everything. They cannot be wrong. That cannot be true.

I know from my experience that sometimes folks with unkind, harmful beliefs do not know any better. Sometimes they are surrounded by people and places who only tell one story, and they crave security and solace from their fear, so they wear their beliefs like armor and they cannot be reached until they are forced into being vulnerable. Maybe they cannot be reached until they feel safe enough to confront old fears. Many people, no matter how well-off they are, will be afraid of the monster under their bed until the day they die.

I don't know what to do with this information. It is not fair to excuse people's hurtfulness because they cannot cope with the pain of realizing their lives are built on a lie. They must still be responsible for who they have been and what they have done. They still must be called to change. And yet, is it fair to demand of people the very behavior they are hardwired against? How can we expect people to know about themselves a thing that they cannot, or to learn a lesson before they have the tools to do so? All of us know how stark and terrifying it is when the world is suddenly unfamiliar and strange, and we are facing it alone.

I suppose my point is that we must try to be as compassionate as we can while upholding as much justice as we can.

While I'm a very different person now, my past is still my past. I cannot absolve myself for the harm I've caused. I cannot forever deny myself compassion, either. I don't expect anyone who knew me then to treat me one way or another. Their beliefs about me are theirs, and I have no claim over them. All I can do is decide how I will treat myself.

I treat myself like this: I forgive myself for what I did when I did not know any better. I offer myself grace and compassion, and I do what I can to apologize to the people I hurt along my path. I have accepted that change is an ever-present process, and I have committed to the act of changing. I try to do things for the right reason. I endure the waves of grief over my lost time. I try to find a home for the anger at how I was mistreated and to let go of the things I wish I could go back and change, but I do not forget the lesson. I can and will be wrong, and if it's fear driving my attachment to an idea, I know I need to be more critical of my own beliefs.

I hope that this story might be helpful for someone who is trying to understand why a certain belief is so hard to shake, for themselves or for someone in whom they want to see the best. I do not suggest it is an excuse, but perhaps it can be another tool we use to see and know each other. Challenging a belief directly might not work, but perhaps we can dig deeper until we find the fear that feeds it. If you can provide a different story that gives the fear a place to be, maybe it won't need to be held onto so dearly. Perhaps if we can prove there is nothing to be afraid of, we can stop making choices in avoidance of pain, and start making choices in pursuit of love.

We are all trying to understand. We all want to feel safe. We are all at the mercy of the information we have. We all must summon great courage to accept the cost of starting anew. We all must stand up for what is right. I can only wish you luck, resolve, and wisdom as we all have the honor of fighting the good fight.

Clementine

I watched someone else peel a clementine—
their hands warming in the window,

and the fine, bright spray that caught the drops of sunlight
as the skin gave way to sour riot inside
reminded me of my life

before you.

The room smelled like summer,
and I swear,
my heart, mind, and soul
were tiny drops of sunlight, too,

and I was free.

For a moment,
warming in the window,
I was free.

you're gonna die alone

Do I want to fall in love?

Sure. Absolutely. I'm on the apps. I'm searching around. I'm giving it a good effort.

But I have a little quirk that I can't quite seem to shake. It's not some attachment disorder, or some too-kinky-too-fast thing, or me asking them to send me $20,000 because my enemies are after me. If you match with me on Tinder, you'll see a couple photos of me doing normal, cute things. Then, when you're about to swipe away, you'll see a photo of me from behind sitting on the edge of a pool, just torso and booty. I won't lie, it's good. Tested and true. And if you look closer, you'll see— just big enough to catch the eye but small enough to make you lean in—my ass tattoo.

In my defense, all I do is set the trap. They walk into it every time.

If you're a man who has matched with me on Tinder, you have officially swiped right. You're looking at the butt-shot, cursing the app for not letting you zoom in. Besotten with the buns, you decide you have to message this siren. You must approach this peachy queen. You want to inquire after the booty, a risky move, as coming on too strong too fast can result in the Great Cockage Blockage. But now you have this tattoo, a little string of numbers— you have found a key. You can skirt the flimsy line of propriety and go straight to the heart of your desires. You can ask about dat ass. You *must* ask about dat ass. You type it out. You press Send.

If you're me, you have just received the same opening message you have gotten a thousand times before.

"What are the numbers tattooed on ya booty?"[1]

Trap? Sprung.

Yes, I want to fall in love—but my fatal flaw is that I'm delighted too thoroughly by my own fuckery to sacrifice the chance to make a funny little joke. So I tell every single one of those curious boys that I have the coordinates to the Declaration of Independence tattooed on my ass.[2]

This splits the men into two categories: those who instantly believe me, and send a Nic Cage GIF or ask if I'm really proud to be an American, and those who think they are smarter than me, so they get reaaaal puffy chested and inform me that my ass tattoo is *not* long enough to be the coordinates to shit.

The Number Twos think they have me cornered. They are waiting for the rewarding pee-pee rush they feel when they have Taught a Woman Something. They stare at their screens expectantly, waiting for my astonished thanks for correcting my silly girl brain. But they do not know that I am the spider, and they have just flown into my itsy-bitsy web.

If there is one thing the type of Tinder-trolling American man who opens with the word "booty" cannot stomach, it is

---

1. See also: ass, dumper, dump truck, dumpy, butt, peach, badonk, etc.
2. I am convinced that the *right* person will be equally as delighted with this fuckery, and so I do not believe I am risking true love. I am only finding it faster.

the idea that a woman knows more about an obscure aspect of the military than he does. So when they tell me my butt tattoo couldn't possibly be the coordinates to a noble document featured in a classic Nicolas Cage blockbuster, I tell them, without blinking, the tattoo is written in a type of military shorthand.

I'm sure they smell bullshit, but they can't call me on it, because *what if I'm not lying?* What if there *is* a type of military shorthand that this fat-assed bitch on Tinder *knows about* and Big Bald Eagle Boy does *not?* They can't risk the embarrassment. They can't risk the shrinkage. And ultimately, they will do anything for the delusional belief that they have a chance to get within exploring distance of my twin suns of Tatooine. So they always, always fold. There are likely hundreds of men walking this earth *right now* who are still unsure if somewhere there is a woman with hella ass marred by a dedication to the founding fathers' scribblings.

As much as I love Nic Cage and a good treasure hunt, I'm not telling these boys the truth. I decided my first tattoo should be my own birthday on my ass while I was on my way to the parlor. I didn't know why I did it at the time. Now I do.

I was not born into a family that encouraged me to be visible, big, or loud. In my family, the women seek to be acceptable, small, and polite. We worship at the altar of palatability, but I wasn't born particularly palatable. My mom will tell you that when I home-base-slid into this world under the glow of *Major League* playing on the hospital room TV, I didn't cry. I just stared at everyone in attendance of my birth, even Charlie Sheen, with an accusatory *"Couldn't this meeting have been an email?"* sort of look. I stand by this behavior.

I was a little girl with a risk-taking, messy, barefoot soul being raised, judged, and loved by the sort of women who fear the unknown. When my family looked at me they didn't see a wide world with endless possibilities, they saw all the things that could go wrong. A little girl who climbed trees was guaranteed to break her neck, so she needed to learn to stay on the ground. I didn't understand why they treated me like a risk. Constantly being critiqued left me hungry for love and acceptance. I always felt like I was being told that being *me* was the wrong thing to be. I just wanted to be enough.

And I was very, very lonely.

I never felt like anyone understood me, and that always felt like my fault. I distinctly remember being warned before hanging out with my crush, "Just, don't be yourself, okay? *Don't be so weird.*" Why couldn't I just be small enough to fit in? Why couldn't I just be normal? Why was I always so *goddamn* much?

I gave little bits of myself away, again and again, offering them up to be tasted and spat viciously back into a bucket. *Too bitter. Too sour. Too cloying.* So I adjusted the recipe. I changed the way I looked, I changed the way I talked, and I changed the way I spent my time. I gave up the things I loved. I stopped climbing trees. I stopped eating more than a thousand calories a day. I gave up, I gave up, I gave up until there wasn't anything left that belonged to *me.* I'd become public property, and I didn't have a drop of unconditional love to show for it.

When I got my own birthday tattooed on my body, I was finally deciding to say, "*I belong to me.*" It was the beginning of my understanding that I'd been searching for love in the wrong places. No one would ever be able to love me in the way I needed. No one was coming to fill the cracks in my heart, to seep into me and regrow the missing pieces. Who was going to take that little kid's face in their hands and breathe belief and abandon and bravery back into her?

No one was ever going to be able to do enough for me. I would never be satisfied.

Because the love and acceptance I needed—the cheerleader,

confidant, hero, and soft place to land I was desperate for—had
to come from me. I was the only one who could collect all the
missing pieces. I was the only one with a map.

I slowly learned that my expectations for others were too
high. I used to believe that expecting the same effort you put into
a relationship back was reasonable. I chose the people I valued
and cherished, then I did what I knew how to do—I overpro-
duced. I went above and beyond. I established an impossible
precedent for who I could be as a friend, and I set my expectations for them just as high. If someone didn't reciprocate what
I'd given so often on the rare occasion I needed it, they were a
bad friend. But with enough time and space and growing up, I
can see that I can only blame myself for the sore heart that comes
when a friend doesn't meet you halfway. I held them against a
sky-high standard they had never agreed to meet.

One day I sat with my Nana on her back patio dipping fries
into ranch and complaining for the hundredth time about how
difficult a certain friend was and how hurt she'd made me feel
again. Nana listened intently, then leaned forward and said,
"Do you think you work so hard to keep this friendship alive
because she reminds you of your parents, and you want to prove
that you can earn that love?"

I wanted to slap my grandma.

When I want to slap random men in bars, it's usually because they're being very wrong. When I want to slap my Nana,
it's usually because she's being very right.[3]

Is there a more slappable offense than someone revealing to
you that you do, indeed, seek out people who are just like your
parents? I'd found people who reminded me of my mom just
so, or my dad just so, and I'd clung to them. I was so worried

---

3. Let it be known I have never slapped my grandma.

about not falling in love with a curly-headed, unibrowed, tanned-and-barefooted drug-addict ninny (sorry, Dad), that I never saw all the other ways we can recreate our parents sneaking up on me. I never suspected to find that dynamic hiding in the creases of the gel-pen-covered notes we secretly passed in class.

When Nana dropped this particular truth bomb, I rejected it. I continued on in my friendships as I had before, expecting different results but experiencing the same resentment and frustration. When my friendships started to buckle and crack under the pressure, I had to reconsider Nana's slap-worthy wisdom. The closer I got to seeing the truth of what I was searching for, the harder it was for those dynamics to hold the weight of my expectations. They could not hold the weight of the lonely, gasping cavern in my heart that always demanded *more*. My friends, no matter how well intentioned, couldn't offer enough to quiet the lonely girl who raged inside of me.

Many of these friends had their own issues, too. It's why they found me, why I found them, and why we were so bonded. I was a fixer, they needed fixing. I was a hero, they needed saving. I was too steady, they were too anxious. I needed to be needed, they needed to be seen. But who can we blame? Aren't we all just hurting kids who need something?

Healing is a messy, painful, and often destructive business.

I don't know a lot, but what I know so far is that I need to be content being entirely, utterly *alone*. If I'm not, it's all going to hurt way too much.

When you think about it, you're the only person you spend every day of your life with. We find the loves of our lives and we lose them. We fall in love, then people change. Our parents die. Our siblings get married and move to somewhere with way too much humidity and an assload of bugs. Our friends change. We change.

We are the person we can count on to pick us up and put us back together again. *We* are the person who always shows up, who washes our hair and does our laundry and cooks us meals. *We* give us the permission to book the flight, say yes to the job in a brand-new place, name our babies after ourselves,[4] or to walk away. The only person who I can bet on to show up, always and forever, is me.

For the sake of argument, let's say I get lucky and die so old I look like I'm an apple that was left in the sun. I bit the dust hand in hand with my lover, still hot at an ancient age, and who happens to be dying at the exact same time. Our family stands around us, thankful for everything we gave them, and gently smiling as we drift away. Let's say we're living the dream of any girl who grew up during Nicholas Sparks's chokehold-on-Hollywood era, and we're about to *The Notebook* this shit into the afterlife, but without the dementia.

When I take my last breath and face the other side, my lover isn't holding my hand anymore.

I'm alone. I'm brand new, and I'm starting again.[5]

If I really want to take my best friend and closest confidant and the Big Love of My Life with me, it better be *me*.

I'm wearing my own birthday on my ass cheek, the way parents tattoo their children's birthdays. The way lovers tattoo their names.

In other words, I care for myself *now*, and *it's enough*.

So I wake up to the sunlight on my face and I open the curtains. I stretch and feel the pull of sleep giving way to day. I run

---

4. I'm a big proponent of women naming their kids after themselves. If I ever have a son, that little sucker is getting named after *me*.

5. Hopefully. If we do just go *poof* and completely cease to exist in any way, I won't be around to realize I got it wrong and no one else will be around to sneer, "*See? Worm food.*" And I'm content with that.

my hands gently over my body and take inventory. I'm all here.

I put on a song that makes me feel like today might be *my day*, and I remember to put on SPF. If I cry, I take the time to feel it and listen to why. If I am walking home and hear live music spilling out of the bar, I ask if I'd like to stop in for a little bit of magic. I splash in puddles, and cook long meals, and I laugh at all my best jokes. If I am overwhelmed, I give myself permission to leave it until tomorrow and I bring myself to bed and rest.

The moments when life grabs me by the shoulders and demands that I rise to the occasion, asking me if I can do it, I remind myself that I *can*. *Of course* I can, because I'm my biggest fan. I'm sitting in the audience of my own preschool play, watching the toddling chaos of a little body trying, and smiling with a bouquet of flowers I can throw at the stage, no matter how far the result was from the plan.

You can be enough for yourself, too.

Because in truth, life is all so sudden. No one is promised anything. Nothing stays for long. I might be the only person who ever wants to ink my existence onto their skin. It might only be me.

It might feel sad, I know, but isn't it also beautiful? The impermanence makes life feel so important and urgent. We only have this moment, so kiss me like you mean it and don't be afraid of what we might lose. We only have this moment, so take my picture while the sun sets over the city skyline.

If you do decide to spend your life searching for the person who will make you feel content, complete, and witnessed, I hope you run into yourself peering through shop windows. I hope you're squinting through the glass with your hands cupped around your face, trying to catch a glimpse of someone promising, longing to be struck by that "*There they are!*" lightning, only to step back and see your own reflection. *There they are.*

For the record, I *also* hope you have the big wild love affair—the Nicholas Sparks, wrap-around-porch, kiss-in-the-rain, If-You're-a-Bird-I'm-a-Bird kind of love, if that's what you want. I hope it inspires novels, and documentaries, and single-handedly powers the next NASA space launch. *Not* the next private launch, because eff all those billionaires shopping for their next planet after they torch this one. In fact, I hope your love affair is so incredibly epic, beautiful, and easy that it ushers in an era of peace in which not a single billionaire exists.

I also hope that when it ends, you find yourself still cradled and comforted by the love of your life: *you.* I hope you enjoy your company and believe that it can be enough when everything else is lost. Being alone and not being lonely is contentment, isn't it?

You don't have to tattoo your own birthday on your ass cheek, but I hope you don't waste any more time trying to find someone else to complete you. I hope you spend every day of your life with your favorite person, and I hope you die alongside them, too.

After all, we're all gonna die alone.

When you think about it, can't that be kind of wonderful?

Closure

When I decided I'd write,
I knew I'd have to step into old rooms
where all of you have spent the night.

I thought I might end up talking to your ghosts too long,
or moving back in,
or painting *I Miss You* in the dust with my fingertip and
     waiting for your reply—

and I know we don't talk anymore,
but can I tell you one last thing?

I typed the final line
and then
I just walked out,
and closed the door behind me.

I poured myself a glass of water,
and I listened to the birds outside,
and I wondered if it might rain this week.

emo kids, daffodils
& microdosing tragedy
as a practice in survival

I'm so sad I was shit at keeping a diary.

I wish I had been better at recording my thoughts, because despite my absolute noodle brain and collection of journals half-started, what I do have proves that teenage me was onto something.

Between the heavy-handed doodles of crying eyeballs and frantically scratched to-do lists that compose my journals, I tried my hand at poetry. My life as a teenage poet was, apparently, very dramatic, and very, very morose. It didn't matter that I went to youth group three times a week, or that I painted my room neon green, pink, and orange—in the hidden pages of my inner world, I was an emo kid.

When I first heard emo and pop-punk music, stolen from the iPod of a friend who sang along with swear words and watched *Invader Zim*, I felt like I was getting away with murder. Screaming boymen in black eyeliner with straightened bangs and Midwestern daddy issues were not a welcome presence in my house. My house didn't have any copies of the *Harry Potter* films, Disney's *Hercules*, or even *The Hunchback of Notre Dame*. I distinctly remember my mother reading aloud the hand-wringing review of *Shrek* from Focus on the Family before I was given permission to see it in theaters. There was a dead body in the castle, presumably the victim of Dragon-with-the-good-lashes, and that was just in the first few minutes. That wasn't even *considering* the many excellent innuendos that were guaranteed to turn your child into a victim of the Ogre Agenda. So I kept my angsty secret to myself, listening to Fall Out Boy, My Chemical Romance, and Simple Plan through headphones, and never singing along where my parents could hear.

I was a voracious reader, but only sad books. Real-life stories, made-up heartbreak, and someone always died in the end. I tore through them with a hunger, and each trip to Barnes & Noble resulted in my mother looking at my new book choices with concerned and confused side-eye. When I told my parents I wanted to paint my nails black, they told me I was only allowed if I added some kind of design in another color. Flowers or zebra stripes, they didn't give a holy heck, but never the inky pitch that nubbed the fingers of the spiritually bankrupt.

I only made the mistake of sharing my poetry with them *once*. After a proud recital of my most recent piece, one that had repeated the words bloody, shredded, and tattered at least twice (each), they stared at me, aghast. Then, very quietly, the way one might approach a scared and injured wolf that was caught in a snare, they told me I needed to go to therapy.

I said no thanks, because they just didn't get it. My tragic and embarrassing poetry wasn't a cry for help. I was just drawn to the dark side of life, to the things that are honest and real. I'd always gravitated to the stories of heartbreak, loss, and survival instead of the candy-colored cheeriness of glossy teenage media. Studying the twin force of joy didn't feel like I was confessing some secret sadness. What good did it do to avoid it and pretend it wasn't real? I was a happy person who was going happy places, but I wasn't afraid of the dark. I'd rather have the therapy money go to another all-black outfit or heartbreaking memoir, anyway.

During my senior year of high school, I was overjoyed to enroll in Advanced Placement Art. I'd evolved from only writing concerning stuff to also drawing concerning stuff, and it was the first time I was going to be formally taught. Our teacher was a passionate, offbeat woman, the way most art teachers are, who encouraged us to learn all we could about the artists, painters, and periods we might love. And I was a textbook kiss ass, so I went right home, fired up the desktop, and asked Google, "What are some good paintings?" The screen filled with color, and I scrolled through the results, Van Gogh and Monet, Khalo, Picasso. I loved so many, but my heart skipped a beat when I first saw *Narcissus* by Caravaggio.

Narcissus depicts the tale of the man by the same name who could not be tempted with beauty until he met his own reflection in the water. Upon glimpsing his face, he fell so deeply in love that he stayed there, pining for himself, neglecting what he needed to survive, until he wasted away. Caravaggio's portrayal is a canvas drenched in black as a man hovers over dark water. Narcissus is the only object in the painting that is cast in light, and as he crawls in high contrast from the background to behold himself, even his reflection is dark and unforgiving— only truly clear in the highlights mirroring the brightest parts of the suffering man.

I was hooked. I learned that Caravaggio was a pioneer of a painting technique born in Italy called chiaroscuro. *Chiaro* means *light* and *oscuro* means *dark*. Chiaroscuro went on to inspire artists across Europe and later across the globe, activating something primal with its brutal, honest contrast—its celebration of the struggle between the clashing forces. There is often only a single, small light source, fighting against the consuming dark to illuminate the subject who persists. So many gallery walls today are adorned with brooding, moody stories still told with the lilt of *Narcissus*.

Many would argue that the style is fundamentally melancholy, dark, and morose. If Caravaggio had been my parents' child, he'd be spending one night a week on an overstuffed armchair being asked, "And how does that make you *feel?*" Blame the emo kid in me, but I simply can't agree. When I stand in front of the portraits of people looking alone in dark rooms, draped in deep velvets or naked and cold, emerging from the depths around them to say, *I am still here*, it is pure hope. It is rebellion. It is the insistence that despite the swallowing background, the candlelit dungeon, or the gaping dark of a moonless forest, the subject still *belongs*. They are to be witnessed. They will not be swallowed, too.

Life imitates art, or art imitates life, whichever chicken or egg you prefer. Being human is a collision of strokes of greatness and strokes of loss, strokes of love and strokes of anger, and a lot of those things are ones we do not get to choose. Sometimes the colors and textures that dominate our canvases are painted into the scene against our greatest effort. We go through life the best we can, but when we step back to admire our work in progress, we can be surprised by overbearing swaths of turmoil threatening to extinguish the nuance and truth of us. We will all see the day each of us becomes the subject of a painting like this. The darkness comes, and when it does, how do we survive?

There aren't many places or people who will tell you that dwelling on the negative is a good way to live, and I agree. I'm not arguing for swapping out our affirming morning mantras with "LIFE IS POINTLESS AND NO ONE GETS ME." But I do think there's an argument for spending enough time reflecting on the fullness of our human experience that in the disorienting moment of blackout, our eyes can adjust to the dark. To indulge in cliché, we do have the power to transform our painful things into redemptive ones. The art of coaxing a subject out of the background to stand in defiant hope is one we will all attempt. So we ask ourselves, as we take in the unbalanced canvas that has suddenly leaned too dark, where can we place a bit of lightness? Where can we interrupt the patch of ink to bring forth the shape and texture underneath? Can we find a single thread of joy amongst the pain? Can we place a sprinkling of humor like starlight—laughter scattering across a now beautiful night sky?

It does not have to be a floodlight that banishes the shadows far away from us. Most of the time when we are drowning in hardship, flipping on a super-mega-watt-bat-signal level light beam is really not an option. Who's going to suddenly jump out of bed and go from deeply depressed to head-cheerleader peppy on the power of their will alone? I don't know anyone like that, and I'm not sure I'd be able to be friends with them if I did. My kind of people are more likely to call eating a vegetable for the first time in a week an extraordinary win. My kind of people weren't very shiny and glossy in high school, and they definitely have sad, poorly written poetry hidden somewhere they hope polite company will never, ever find. But I'd bet on the lady with the three-day-old bun and the playlist of teen angst anthems over the one who pretends the hard days never come. If there's anything the thousands of brilliant artists who came before us proved, it is that the smallest flicker of light can be enough to render, from a darkness that feels all-encompassing, a masterpiece.

I believe in laughing at ourselves and the things we cannot control so consistently that it feels second nature if devastation knocks on our door. I believe in watching sad movies, reading sad books, and letting the emotions wash over us to teach us something before they settle back home. Learning how to understand how we feel and react in the face of great suffering is like learning how to paint before you attempt a master canvas. I've watched a lot of people who were relentlessly positive crumble when the darkness came because they had never looked it in the eyes before. They'd never accepted it was possible. They'd never learned its name. The people who know that heartbreak is inevitable, and who have spent time witnessing the many ways that humans do and do not cope might be more prepared. They have studied the many masterpieces left behind by those who came before. They have practiced pressing light into dark canvases. The emo kids might, actually, be pretty well adjusted.

I think of *Narcissus*, the stunning portrait of a boy who confused self-love for self-sabotage, and I think I am much the same. I have avoided what I should have embraced out of a misguided sense of self-protection, of self-care, and it has been my downfall. We face the same choices that people have since thousands of years ago. We tell the stories of their wins, as well as their losses, which are, perhaps, more valuable, and we let their failures be a study in the vicious contrast of dark and light. The result is striking. Important. Valuable. A guide to our own opportunity. A map to find our way out.

The story of Narcissus is meant to be a warning, a dark and tragic tale, but what it has inspired and birthed in its wake has been remarkable. In some accounts, Narcissus's story is actually one of hope. Some say the beautiful, tragic boy didn't simply waste away to nothing but was transformed into a bright, resilient flower. A flower that blooms no matter how roughly it is treated. Genus name, *Narcissus*, commonly known as the daffodil. In Victorian England's language of flowers, where each flower had a meaning, to give someone a daffodil often symbolized the gift of *new beginnings*.

Not everyone needs to think Wednesday Addams is an icon, but perhaps we learn to practice the art of finding humor in the sad poetry, of finding release in the angsty lyric, of finding familiarity in the tearful watch of a big-screen tragedy. Perhaps we can witness depictions of hardship with curiosity and the willingness to share a small bit of the sting. I hope for us all that when the big one knocks on our door, we have a certain muscle memory. We've heard its stories and its purpose, so it is easier for us to start to find our way out. To start again. Only a flicker of light is enough to emerge from our dark forest, to insist, stubborn and brave: *I will not be swallowed. I will be witnessed. I'm still here. I'm still here.*

Self-Portrait

the crumple of paper as you turn a new page
when a dog puts its paw on your foot
rounding the corner where someone waits in Arrivals
the "EXACTLY!" of the understood

the bittersweet smell of a place you once loved
October crows scattering into flight
the taste of fresh butter on sourdough toast
the animal thrill of the fight

laughter pouring out of an open pub door
the shadow of lines long erased
sewing a button back onto a bear
the monster you have yet to face

in defense of pigeons: the case for mercy

Unpopular opinion: I love pigeons.

I mean it. I *love* them. I love their fat little bodies and their mangled little feet and all the colors they come in. I mean seriously, have you ever seen one of those brown-and-white ones? They look so chic—like they have entire closets of camel-toned capsule wardrobe pieces. Like they are always dressed for a quick cappuccino at a sidewalk café in Italy. Gorgeous.

Yet, despite being both Miss America and Miss Congeniality material, pigeons are largely hated. People think they're gross, invasive, and only around to cause problems. They think pigeons ugly and ordinary. But why? We all love a pheasant, right? Wow, what a stunner, huh? What an illustrious bunch of plumage! A feathered trophy! We *adore* a pheasant! Well, guess what? Pigeons have the same colors as pheasants,[1] you dip.

It's not the inspiring colors, though, that have turned me into a self-proclaimed champion of pigeonkind. I love them

1. Kinda.

because they are the unequivocal underdog of the bird world.[2]

So many of us people have rotten opinions of the little birds, but I wonder if we've each chosen that opinion for ourselves, or if we have been trained to see them this way. Pigeons didn't ask to be under our feet on Manhattan sidewalks—they didn't even ask to be in the United States! Colonizers brought them to be our companions. We forced them to make a home in the "new world."[3] We got them hooked on the hustle and bustle of city life, feeding them delightful cuisine that made them all fat and happy and getting them accustomed to a certain level of high living. People relied on pigeons to keep up our affairs and share our sentiments. We tied love notes and hate notes to their feeties to fly around to our hookups and nemeses, and we fed them treaties when they got home for doing a super good job. I'm positive there is more than one pigeon in history who has been a shoulder to cry on for a heartbroken socialite. "Oh, Plucky, how *could* he? How could he run off with that harlot? Stay away from jazz and liquor, Plucky! Stay away from jazz and liquor!"

We took them from their homes, built them into our lives as integral friends, companions, and daily facets of being, and then we abandoned them.

Now they're the victims of a vicious smear campaign. Pigeons are trying to figure out life without the people and comforts they were brought to know; we're all busy sullying their good name. You'll hear about donut-stealing pigeons, dirty and covered in mysterious grimes and goops, caking the ethereal beauty of the world's most important cities in literal shit.

---

2. You could make an argument for chickens. RIP the many nuggies I have consumed.

3. It should be noted there was very much already a whole ass world full of all kinds of people and cultures before Europeans showed up with pigeons and the genocidal notion of Manifest Destiny.

But take a step back and think about the accusations that supposedly make pigeons worthy of revile. Crowding, taking, littering? That sounds pretty familiar, no? Eating trash, living on a prayer, packed into a tiny, shoebox dwelling in a high-rise, and having suffered a light maiming in pursuit of big-city dreams? Everyone I've ever known who moved to New York City can be described in this *exact* same way.

Meanwhile, pigeons stay softly nestled high in the intricate New York skyline—dotting the iconic sight with handmade dwellings that remind them of the tall cliffs back home. They just want a full belly. They just want a safe little life. How does that sound different than most of us out here struggling? I bet somewhere far back in their bones they remember when people used to be their friends, so they aren't very scared of us.

They end up under our feet, and we kick them. Imagine being brought somewhere you never asked to be then being so viscously resented for being there?

My favorite poem is one by Rudy Francisco—a genius—that I came across on Facebook many years ago, back when I had a Facebook.[4] I reposted it every time I saw it because it reminded me to be the sort of person I am trying to grow into. It is called "Mercy," and in it the poet describes his choice to relocate a spider outside using the "most peaceful weapons" he can find instead of opting to kill it. He hopes that if he finds himself in the same position as the spider, wrong place, wrong time, he can also count on mercy.

(I cannot go on without acknowledging that the poet is a Black man in America, and I imagine he has a very different reason to be hoping for mercy than someone like me. In fact, someone like me is the reason someone like him might be forced to hope for mercy.)

---

4. This dates me.

Sometimes I think back to the many times in my life I opted for a shoe instead of a cup and paper. I remember the times I chose a heart that was hard and entitled—when I believed that I had the right to decide which creature belongs and which one doesn't.[5] I wish it wasn't true, but I haven't always reached for mercy when given the choice. Sometimes I still don't.

I also wonder about the times that I have found myself the spider. The pigeon. Those times that I somehow survived being in the wrong place at the wrong time. It's a miracle I've encountered mercy more than once. So many of us are not met with peaceful weapons.

And so, in defense of pigeons, maybe we could think twice before we kick after their little, waddling selves. Maybe we could try to not take their lack of personal space or their pizza-crust lust personally. We could shoo them on kindly, and wish them well. Perhaps it would do all of us good to reacquaint ourselves with the opinions we accept as our own and interrogate their origins. We may even find a friend in what we once believed was a foe. I would even say you could share your pizza with a new feathered friend, but I think it's not great for their systems.[6] I doubt a New York slice is native to their high rocky cliffsides.

I hope somewhere tonight a pigeon has gone through its whole day without being scared for its tiny, feathered soul. It should have a full belly, and a happy thought in its little head, and perhaps it might be curious about what a cloud could be. I hope it flies home to a warm nest, where it coos softly with a bird it is quite fond of as it watches the sun go down over the

---

5. This is probably in large part due to my whiteness, which insists incorrectly that white people have the right to decide who belongs and who doesn't. (This is so fucked up and incorrect.)

6. I, too, cannot resist a good slice of pizza, despite it wreaking havoc upon *my* soft little bod.

Hudson, high above the city. I hope it falls asleep thinking whatever way that pigeons think about the magic of the changing sky.

And somewhere far down below, I hope one of us humans watches the same sky streak magnificent. I hope we are filled with wonder and our breath catches just a tiny bit as we take in the ordinary miracle. And perhaps at that moment, we notice a spider high in the corner of the room building a sturdy web, or a pigeon lands on our windowsill. I hope with all my heart we think fondly of the littler creatures, doing their best to live and work and find their place in a world that keeps changing, and we simply carry on with our own business. I hope we keep choosing mercy. I hope we receive it, too.

Poem for a Child

You were born a brilliant, gentle, and desperate thing
who loved all the small bugs,
and promised much older people they were going to be okay.

You were a good person,
but that's not what you heard:
tantrum girl with her stubborn will and her selfish,
    sword-point tongue.

You—so ungrateful.

I wish I could go back with you now
to put a crown on your head,
cupcakes on your table, paint your nails black, and say:

I have never seen such a glorious thing:
first-rain-of-autumn, fire-licked girl with her ever-soft hands
    and her warrior heart.

You—so impossible.

You—so unbeatable.

You:
so good
so good
so good.

the most powerful question in the world

You know how in job interviews you get to the end, and your hands are still shaking and you've blacked out for the last twenty minutes and you have no idea what day it is, then the big boss interviewer asks, "Do you have any questions for me?"

I have a hack for this. A killer question. An ace in the hole. It can turn you from a bumbling hobbit who keeps dropping all their snacks to a veritable Gandalf in a job interview.[1]

When an interviewer asks me if I have any questions, I always respond, "If you woke up tomorrow and everything was perfect, what would have changed overnight?"

Boom.

Yeah, it freaks them out. It also makes them look at you like, "*Woah, that's one insightful and confident motherfucker.*"[2]

It's not just job interviews. I use this question in my most

---

1. I once tried to read *The Hobbit*, and it took them so fucking long to get out of the Shire I couldn't do it. Like, get your bumbly shit together, hobbits. Further the plot.
2. They don't expect you to be like "how is your life sad?" You know? They never see it coming.

high-stakes get-to-know-yous. If I'm on a crunched time limit, trying to crack a particularly difficult nut, invested in getting right past the barriers, propriety, or the fear of vulnerability, I bust this out.

I picked up this question from my favorite professor. She was, in my experience, a fucking genius, and I took every class she offered. In my Helping Relationship class, my professor offered this question as a way to get through the barriers of establishing a new relationship with a therapeutic client. Someone coming to therapy might not know what to say—they only know they are in pain. Asking "what brings you in?" won't get you far, but this question can. This question can shake loose the old gunk clogging up a heart.[3]

If you woke up tomorrow and everything was perfect, what would have changed overnight?

The most revealing part of this question is sometimes *how* someone chooses to answer. Will they talk about world hunger? Racism? Capitalism? Will they talk about the new pair of shoes they want, or being on a boat in Corfu, or driving off the lot in a Tesla? Or will they talk about peace, loss, love, and a cure for the lonely heart?

I don't know if anyone has ever asked *me* this question—it's my move, after all. If I were asked, I think I could answer it in every single way and I'd still be telling the truth.

If you ask me for the big picture, I would end racism and white supremacy and all the bullshit that springs forth from

---

3. The final for this class was a ten-minute therapy session with the professor, in which she would pull a character with an issue out of a hat, and your entire class would sit on the other side of one-sided observation glass and take vigorous notes on how deeply you would have scarred your client if it had been a real therapy session. One girl had a panic attack and tried to run through the sliding glass doors in the room, only to realize one second too late that they were still, tragically, closed. I tried to give her a passing grade anyway.

their rancid little pond.[4] A lot of things would fall into place after that. Capitalism would crumble, people would eat, people would have a warm place to sleep.

If you ask me for material things, I'd tell you I wish my apartment had more natural light. Actually, I'd own multiple apartments all across the globe in my favorite cities, all flooded with daylight and all full of love and life even when I'm not there. There would be sustainable high fashion for plus-size people and it would be affordable. I wouldn't be allergic to gluten or dairy anymore. I'd spend a lot of time in the sun eating cheese, and a lot of time in the rain eating cheese, and I'd always have access to a boat on the water with a sundeck calling my name. I'd probably tell you I could teleport, but that's not very much in the spirit of the question, so I'd take it back. I'd have a few good friends I could always call. I think I'd have a great dog that was easy to travel with, and a fulfilling career that made a difference, and I'd maybe have gorgeous dark-red hair and wear silk slip skirts and be fabulously wealthy when I came home for Christmas.

But if you ask me about the real things, the sort of things that might *actually* make life perfect if they changed, I'd have to think a little harder.

To be completely honest, I'm a guilty girl with two hearts. I've always felt this way, and maybe you do too. When I take quizzes about who I'd be in a movie or what type of bread I'd be, I feel like I'd be equal parts of most. I'm half brain and half brawn. Part mage and part warrior. I've always felt like I'm not a firebender or a waterbender, but the Avatar themselves.[5] I'm

4. I'm pretty convinced that most evils come back to that. White Supremacy and Patriarchy and Money are hard to start pulling apart, but their horrible kids are ableism and xenophobia and fatphobia and transphobia and homophobia and biphobia and, and, and . . .

5. *Avatar: The Last Airbender* is an EPIC show. It was written for kids, but it's packed full of the heart and wisdom that adults have often forgotten. I

half creative and half logical. I see every side to every problem. I carry two truths all the time.

I tell you this so you can understand—I have a truth that I know is true, and a truth that I *feel* is true. Sometimes they coincide, and sometimes they really don't. I sit here and write to you, pouring out my biggest lessons and learnings and all the ways I'm so happy and free on my own, but I sometimes still cry in the shower over how hard it is to be alone. They exist together, holding hands, deep in my chest.

So if you were to ask me, "If you woke up tomorrow and everything was perfect, what would have changed overnight?" and you wanted the real, deep, honest truth, you would get one of two answers.

If you caught me on a raw heart day, deep in the pain and worry, I might tell you I'd have someone to love me. I might tell you that I was sick of doing it all on my own, and that it's really fucking hard to be single, and that my god wouldn't it be wonderful to have someone else to fold the fucking laundry? Wouldn't it be wonderful to have someone else to watch my life unfold and make me feel like it was real? I might tell you that I write poems about living an unseen life, that I bitterly miss the moments that once felt like love, and that I'm tired of cursing the names of the people who left me behind. If you caught me on a raw heart day, I might tell you that my life would be perfect if I didn't have to work and someone else took care of me from sunup to sundown. I might tell you that I'm so tired of being tired, and I just want to finally know what it feels like to be *chosen*.

I think my friends who haven't been single for more than a few months here or there for most of their adult lives have no

---

believe we should all watch that little beauty.

fucking idea how hard it is to be on your own. They don't know how hard it is to choose yourself because no one else is going to, or at least when there's no proof that you're choosable. And I don't think they have any idea what it feels like to have to make every meal themselves, and then do all the freaking dishes too.

If you asked me on a raw heart day what would make my life perfect, I might say that my family wouldn't have any weird toxic bullshit swirling around, that my siblings would call more often, and that my grandma wouldn't make a single comment about her weight at dinner. Eventually, I'd loop back around every time to being cared for and loved and cherished.

In short, my raw heart would wonder out loud what it might be like to live the life of more beautiful women. More gentle women. Women who are so much easier to love.

Sometimes it makes me feel like a fraud. As I've been writing this book and being visible on the internet, I've been dogged by the feeling that the other shoe is about to drop. I've said to a friend, "I feel like any day now they're all going to realize it's a lie, and I'm making it all up." To which my friend said, "What the hell are you talking about? It *is* you, and it *is* your life, and I'll testify." I think what I meant is: I feel like if you caught me on a raw heart day, I couldn't practice what I preached.

But then I remember that no one, no matter how saintlike and centered and emotionally well they may be, can live every day as their best self. We're all just little bottles of space stuff and blood and effort, and some days we turn out a bit more animal than celestial. That's okay. Something very wonderful about being human is that you can be doing your best, and that can be enough. It can be enough for someone else, too.

All that said, if you were to catch me on a day where I felt at home in my heart (I hope it's fair to say this is most days), I would have a different answer.

On a full heart day, I'd tell you that if I woke up tomorrow and my life was perfect, I would have finally ditched the last trailing fingers of fear. Nothing and no one would be plucking at loose threads, stoking the terror of it all falling apart. I'd be brave all the time, and I'd be free all the time, and I wouldn't be afraid of losing the things that were mine.

On a full heart day, if I woke up to a perfect life, I would be completely open to falling in love. I wouldn't be afraid of the fallout of a broken heart. I'd be looking forward to the wild wonder of discovering someone new. I'd know that I'd be okay when they came, and I'd be okay when they left, and I'd learn all about life and myself in the meantime.

If I woke up tomorrow and life was perfect, I'd be calling opportunities to me with all the confidence of someone who believes they deserve them. I wouldn't be the first one to tell myself that something was too big for me. I'd leave that to people with much smaller imaginations than I have.

I think I'd say that I'd be comfortable, and I'd have lots of friends who liked to come over and have dinner while we listen to the waves below, and I'd know how to do card tricks and mix the perfect cocktail and knit really large, soft blankets very quickly.

When I stop to reflect on these two different hearts and their two different answers, I notice one thing very clearly. On a full heart day, my perfect life is really just a series of small choices away. I can choose to ignore the fear, I can choose to give myself permission, and I can choose to chase after new love with abandon. I can invite a friend over for drinks, and while it might not be perfectly mixed, and while we might be listening to the sound of traffic instead of the sea, it's pretty damn close. I can learn how to mix a drink. I can find my way to the water.

And the raw heart days? They pass. They do come, and for

a moment I'm just another little animal doing my best down here on this spinning rock—lonely and prone to believing lots of other people's stories about what is and isn't real. But then the hard days pass, and I wake up at home in my heart again, and I remember that I'm an author now. I'm writing my own stories about what matters.

We all are.

So I invite myself—and you—to consider the following:

If you woke up tomorrow and your life was perfect, what would have changed overnight?

And maybe, more importantly, *how much of that do you already have control over?*

Bad Habits

Of all my bad habits,
that will drive you insane,
I'll keep the worst one hidden the longest.
And long after you've told me
to stop picking my skin,
leaving cupboards open,
and stealing the covers,
you'll realize the worst habit of all
is that I won't believe you
when you tell me that you love me.
I'll tell you to stop.
I'll try to prove you wrong.
But I hope you'll stick with it,
and you'll tell me again,
and again,
until *I love you* doesn't sound like a threat.
Because if there's one thing I do believe?
It's that bad habits can be broken.

a confession to my lover (should i ever find you)

To my lover,

I am afraid I'll never meet you, or worse, that I have missed you. What if you were right there with me but I couldn't see— so intent on watching my own unsteady feet? I am afraid that you have thought *she might be the one*, but I have made you wait too long for a person who is ready—so you have found another.

And if we haven't met before, will you know me when you see me? Will you sense the world I'll spin you out of my untapped, still-brave heart? Or will you miss me under the clouds sewn from my bitter distrust, so thick they block the sun?

I hope with all my heart that we will find a way. However long we have, and wherever we may be, I'll take it. I'll take every minute.

I want to feel the feeling of someone wanting me, choosing me, and loving me so kindly. But I confess, it is not the greatest reason that I hope we come together. Sometimes I'm afraid that you are the key to the thing I want the most.

What if the best version of me cannot be born until I find you?

I *am* happy without you. I am my own favorite person, and

I give myself the world, but it is not the same as being allowed to love somebody else. Anyone who says so is a liar. Anyone who says so is afraid.

I might be scared, but I am always trying to be honest.

I think the Me I like the most is the one who is in love, but I need to find you to prove it.

I cannot stop to think too much about what I would do if I had you here. All the ways I'd care for you—the way I'd pass my days. It makes me heartsick for a life I do not have. It makes me miss you, and I do not think we've met.

But it is not only the things I cannot do and the life we cannot build that make my heart ache with longing. I don't believe that anyone completes anyone else, and I know I am already whole, but I cannot unlock every door in the hallways of my life. Some versions of us can only open when we find the key, and sometimes the key is in the shape of someone else.

I am afraid I might only bloom in love.

I sometimes feel like I'm living my life in only half its color. When I watch or read other people's love stories, I covet that they are something beautiful and mad. They can act like children. They can play. They can exchange their loves and fears and bodies with abandon. They can make rash choices in pursuit of desires of the heart, and no one feels the need to stop them.

There are very few places a girl can be so free. So many of the things you can do when you're in love are called mania when you're alone. I want to be reckless. I want to be childish. I want the permission of your love to unlock somebody new.

While there are some versions of me I hope I never have to meet—like the one who's lost someone too young, or the one who's been betrayed—I cannot wait to discover who I am in honest love. Who can I become wrapped in that sort of safety—that sort of support—that sort of camaraderie? Who can I become with someone else choosing me to spend their time with and seeing the very best in me? Sometimes I miss her, even though we haven't met.

Without You, I cannot know Me. I can only dream and speak to possibility. So I pray I meet You, and in doing so, meet Me too. Where else can I bring all of this special creativity and passion? Curiosity and joy? I want to be able to do things for another, to coax the wonder from your heart like I deal in magic. I'll fill your world with color, with life, with music. I'll make my heart the safest place on Earth for you to call home.

When I meet you, I promise, I will help you unfold all of your layers. I will help you find every single part of you that's been waiting to come alive. I will make sure it's getting sunlight, and that it isn't overwatered, and that our cat isn't eating any leaves when we aren't looking.[1]

All I ask is that you do the same for me. If finding you could finally move the most stubborn parts of my heart that have not learned to trust, there might be no limits to who I could become. I want to throw open the door and find in me somebody new. I want to be cast in gentle sunlight, planted in earth, steady and honest enough to bloom.

> In the tender hope
> that I may find you,
>
> Me

---

1. I'm really allergic to cats though, so . . . that's a hard maybe.

Little Girls

Of all the reasons it's a shame
we force little girls to be mothers
the worst of them all must be:
Mothers who never get to grow up
bury their little girl ghosts
in the little girl bones
of their daughters.

to my mother's
inner child

To My Mother's Inner Child,

I've started and restarted this letter what feels like a thousand times, but there's no way I can keep you from getting angry, and there's no way I can get it all right. I have to say this, but I'm sorry if it hurts. I hope it passes quickly. Maybe this will break open the darkness, bring in the sun and fresh air, and let the wounds breathe. Maybe, though the first sting of it all will be sharp, it will yield to peace in the places that have only known the sound of riot.

I hope this letter finds the secret door, weaves through the brambled plane of time, and collapses the space between us to land in the hands of the little girl who will grow up to be my mom. I hope that little girl is reading this now. I have a message for you.

I know that you spend many of your days believing that you are not good enough. It is the ghost in every room that nobody else can see. The thought that you have fallen short gnaws at your heart and burns into shame—shame so hot and dangerous it feels like it could kill you—so you covet it and protect it. No one can know you are a failure, so you do anything you have to to hide the terrible truth—things that do not always make you proud, but they keep you safe. Your whole life you've just wanted to be safe.

If I could say something simple to soothe your fearful soul, I would tell you every day. But the truth is, when something like that is buried so deeply in our bones, nobody else's words can scrub it off. Words are a temporary salve at best—the fleeting relief of a cool rag on a fevered forehead. I cannot hold a compress to the fevered soul. That, little girl, comes down to you.

I am only here to help. So let me tell you what I know, since I've known you my whole life, and together we might find the place that can peel the world wide open.

What I know about you is that it wasn't your fault—the way that the adults who were supposed to love you let you down. They abandoned your heart because *they* fell short. They didn't want to hurt you, but parents can be selfish, and parents can be wrong, and parents' love for their children does not always transcend everything else. Parents were once wounded as little ones too. Sometimes their pain can sneak right past them, into their love, and jump the line to you.

Did you know I've met your mother? I knew her mother too, and I know your arms must be tired. You've been dragging the hope chest, passed from your mother to you, around for so many years. It's full of the inheritance only the daughters endure, heavy and gnarled and born so long ago. Every mother who came before you added her own weight to the pile. You must be exhausted. My arms are tired too.

The women in our family learn a cruel kind of magic—to wrap their soft hearts around their shame and crystallize their muscle into resentful, bitter stone. Though it may look different for each one of us, the same Fear is to blame. It is the thing that lives in the hope chest. Sometimes it's angry, loud, demanding—the Fear that commands like a queen. Sometimes it's meek, a victim of the world—the Fear that cowers and demands to be saved. Sometimes it's vicious, a wounded dog being cornered—Fear that bites when it was wagging its tail only moments before. It has many faces, but only one name: the Fear of Being Left Behind.

You should not have been made to spend so much of your life afraid. Guarding the hope chest of intergenerational worry is not a job for a little girl. It's not true that we will only love you until you let us down.

The Fear will follow you into adulthood. It will keep you from dreaming too big, or climbing too high—always whispering in your ear, *You are bound to fall. You are bound to fail.* You will believe it, because your mother taught you, like her mother taught her, to listen to its voice. The hope chest in the corner of your heart will thrum with the warnings of the women who came before you, waiting to be passed to your little girl. No one ever tells you you're allowed to break the chain.

I know you always wanted to be a mother—tucking your dolls into bed every night so they could get good rest. Someday you will grow up and have a daughter who will inherit the things that you must pass down—the daughter you will teach to speak the language of the ones who made you *you.*

So you will give her the hope chest—her birthright—and hope it is something you can use to relate. It is full of tradition and a secret way to pass wisdom. It is the way we have all survived so far.

At first, she'll take it proudly. All she'll ever want is to be enough and make you proud. And while it's true that you've always been proud of her, she won't know that for a very long time. How could you say it? How could she hear it? There are no words for *You're perfect to me,* and *You don't need to change a thing about yourself* in the language we speak between mothers and daughters.

You will feel like she is a challenging child and won't know how to handle a girl who is so different from you. She will be born with adventure raging inside her and the need to feed her lion's heart. Her courage will make you so very proud, but also very afraid.

Because you learned from *your* mother: girls who speak the language of boldness get their tongues cut out. Ones who leap from tall places break their bones. Those who make life too hard are easier to abandon. Women, in the world you were raised in, have to be palatable to survive, and you will need her to *survive*.

So you will do your best to impress upon your little girl the importance of the hope chest and what lives inside. Fear keeps you *safe*, after all. You will try to teach her to carve down and tamp out the parts of her that set her apart from a crowd. A little pain now, a lot of pain saved later when Failure comes to collect. You will put her in dresses, and tug a brush through her hair, and squeeze her feet into frilly white socks. When you were a baby your mother taped bows to your bald head so that people knew you were a girl. You had your share of ruffle socks too, and here you are—alive.

But your daughter will hate the feeling of those socks around her ankles. She will itch for the cool grass crushed beneath her as she races the crows taking flight. She will want to fall asleep with muddy toes. She will loathe brushing her hair.

The two of you will spend a lot of her life locked in a silent war. You will try to keep her contained, for her safety, *and* for yours, and she will feel the threat to her freedom and fight. You will worry: What will the world think when they see her—unruly body, wild mane, and wicked grin? *What sort of mother lets her daughter be so messy? What sort of mother lets her daughter be so strange?* You will worry the world will smell blood in the water. The wounded dog of your heart will sense danger and snap, and you will forget how easily you can hurt her as you wrestle her toward something passing as pretty. She won't understand why you cannot just love her. You will think, *that is all I am doing*.

You will critique, she will withdraw, and you will regress into the girl who'd rather wound than be left behind. You will try more and more ways to make her shrink, make her stay, and she'll develop a Fear of her own kind. Your daughter will learn that yearning for love only leads to rejection and pain. She will watch the way you love other people so freely, and the anger and jealousy will take root in her heart. While it might feel to you like she gets all of your effort, she will feel like you're far away. Your mother's mother's gift will whisper that she is not good enough to be loved, or to make anyone stay. So her Fear will be the one which is cold and on its own. No one can tell her she's not enough if they aren't close enough to tell. She will be too independent, too severe, too strong. But deep in her heart she will hope it isn't true, so she will also seek out people who will not love her, and try to prove that they can. And she will fail.

You will wonder how your daughter became such a hardened, cold, untouchable thing. She will wonder if there will ever be a day you look at her and find nothing to try to fix. Neither of you will hear, behind your own rising voices, all the mothers' mothers' shouting. You and your daughter will struggle to hear each other at all.

But it is not fear that will be your legacy.

She will watch the way you fiercely defend what you believe is right or wrong. She will watch you go to therapy when it all feels like too much. She will watch you change, grow, and work on who you are, even when other people your age consider themselves done changing. She will watch you make hard choices, again and again, to keep your promises to your family. She will watch the way you wrestle with your pain and fear to build a world of wonder for the children whom you love so much. She will watch you do your best, and mess it up, but never quit. You will pick yourself up, and start again in your work to be the best mom you can be, even if you sometimes believe deep in your heart you might *never* be a good mom. You *never* stop trying. Your daughter will see how hard you have always, always *tried*.

And one day, she will think of what you have taught her while she is lonely with her own secret ghosts—whispering that she would never be good enough to be loved—and she will decide to *try*. She will seek out the parts of her that need to be laid to rest. She will work to build up the bones and muscles she wasn't born with, and ask for the eyes of others when she cannot see herself clearly. She will meet her anger in rooms with the curtains thrown open and ask it for its name. She will say goodbye to the people she has been and lay them down to sleep. She will root out the parts of her heart that have been touched by the creeping cold of her family inheritance, the Fear of being abandoned for not being *enough*, and she will pull them out with her own fingers. She will take those squirming, knotted things into the sun and breathe through the pain of the light burning the darkness away. She will accept that she will have to spend her whole life being aware of the seeds left growing in shadow—parts that will need to be found and offered back to the open air and the light of day. She will accept that life, in large part, is learning to breathe through the pain while we turn our bodies back to the sun. She will accept that life, in large part, is the constant, quiet courage of *trying*.

She will learn that from *you*.

Now your daughter no longer fears being alone. She embraces her time, her own company, and the way she sees the world without anyone to call a partner. You were taught to fight, to force someone to stay, or to make them leave before they can leave you, but your daughter welcomes people into her life, and she lets them go when they want to leave. She has learned to let people pass through her world with grace.

Mom, I broke the chain. I *did it*. I'm free. I'm not afraid of dying alone. I'm not afraid of being left behind. Mom, I am finally *free*.

I'm sorry for the times I couldn't understand you. I had to go through my anger and pain, and you know it hasn't always been easy. But I'm so thankful to you for what you have done to give me my best shot. The older I get, and the more I work on emptying that chest we've always carried with us, the more I can appreciate how hard you have worked already. I'm so sorry for all the extra things that were stacked against you. I'm so thankful that you unpacked as much as you could from that chest before you passed it on. I'll take care of the rest, you don't have to worry. I'll bury it on the hilltop. The hope chest stops with me.

And I know that sometimes you worry you are a disappointment, in the deepest corners of your heart, but you are not a disappointment to me. I am so proud of you.

I didn't always understand, but as my struggle has yielded to compassion, I know how *hard* it is for you to overcome your own mind some days. I know how hard it is for you to live in two worlds, two times—the mother, and the little girl left behind. I know your head can be a place of fear, anxiety, and hopelessness, and I know that *despite* that being your reality, you have never stopped trying to be the best you could possibly be.

Is there anything braver than that? Is there anything that takes more heart and courage than getting back up, again and again, when you are convinced that you are only bound to fail?

To my mother's inner child, you are safe. You are whole. You are good enough. To my mother, thank you.

Your daughter was born with a lion's heart.

She inherited her heart from you.

It Was Good Enough for Me

Recently I was trying to explain to a friend that
I am tired,
and sometimes lonely,
and I am a bit lost,

but if I died tomorrow
I'd be proud of this little life.

I've already taken such a long journey home.
I've already worked so hard to harvest all of this peace.

If I died tomorrow,
this little life I led—
one that many might say was cut tragically short,
all so convinced I was meant for more wonderful things—

would be enough for me.

I was loved,
and I loved, too.
I was happy, and I painted, and I sang.
I fed people warm meals,
and I asked myself if I was kind and if I was brave,
and I helped the birds with broken wings that found me.

I was just one little bit of magic,
doing my very best—
meant for exactly what I had when I had it
and nothing more.

So, hey, don't borrow trouble!
It was good enough for me.

instructions
for my funeral

First of all, someone better water my plants. I worked really hard to keep those alive. Maybe I should have worked harder on me . . . Oops.

Second of all, I have some instructions for how I'd like my funeral to go. I know there are traditions and this and that, but I'm not the traditional sort. Rest assured, if I am dead I am actively haunting you in neutral, hanging around to make sure that you follow my last wishes to a fuckin' T. If you mess this up—my final chance to be a dramatic, showy bitch—I will shift into haunting you in earnest. I will knock *so many things* off your nightstand, so help me god.

Okay, so here are the rules. I am tempted to tell you to bury me in a plastic-lined casket full of ranch dressing and cheese, so I could rest peacefully submerged in what I love. But even the strongest box couldn't keep the bugs out when cheese is on the line, so instead, fire me up, baby. I dyed my ash-blond hair in life. I'll go natural in death.

I want you to get me a sexy-looking black box. It needs a flat enough surface for you all to do the scene from *P.S. I Love*

You. There should be shot glasses next to the box, empty and beckoning, and a full bar with a bartender. One by one, come up, take a shot, and leave that glass upside down on my box. I want the little dribbles of booze to trickle down to me. I want to be a part of the party.

Everybody needs to come looking hot as hell. I want all my single friends to meet and fall in love. I want the sorrow of my passing to leave you all so emotionally exposed, you tumble into each other's arms. Don't get sad when you tell the story of how you met. Tell people your mutual friend set you up. Make sure the venue for my funeral is somewhere with lots of cheeky broom closets and hidden corners where mourners can all make out.

As far as flowers, I don't want any traditional funeral nonsense. If I was married, you can recreate my wedding archway. Put my box and the bar under a cascading arch of blue delphinium and blush ginestra. When everyone gets there, hand each one of them a chocolate cosmo to carry to their seat.[1] They will start to die the second you take them out of water. Good. Let the beauty be so temporary. Let the sugar scent help you say goodbye.

As far as speeches go, send in the fucking clowns—the ones who can tell a sad story with the expert touch of laughter. Think of the times I made you laugh until it hurt. Tell those stories again. Laugh again. Cry if you have to—do them both if it feels right. I know it is not fair of me to ask you not to miss me. But perhaps I can convince you to miss me a little less.

I do not believe that I am somewhere missing you. I think I'm happy, and there is maybe music, and probably the spiritual plane's equivalent of food. I think that where I am, time isn't real

---

1. Chocolate cosmos are tiny, dark maroon and brown flowers with petals that feel like velvet to the touch. They are delicate, and expensive, and their centers smell like Tootsie Rolls.

at all, so nothing feels like so long ago. It does not feel like you have so long to go until you're with me. And while it's probably hard to feel like I am far from you, I hope you can embrace that nothing lasts forever. Sometimes the people that we love are not a northern star, always glowing in our sky. Sometimes we love and laugh and dream alongside people like comets— people meant to blaze a path and then to say goodbye.

If there is one thing I can promise, it's that I don't regret a thing. My life was a wonderful collision of joy and loss and beauty. I'm sorry to the people I hurt—I hope you can forgive me. To anyone who hurt me—it doesn't matter anymore. It hasn't mattered in a very long time. The only thing I want for you is a lifetime full of peace.

To the people who have loved me, thank you for a life so very full of light. Not everyone has the chance to feel the warmth of such incredible humans. I do not take for granted all the ways I have been surrounded, uplifted, and carried. I remember every bowl of soup, every gentle touch, and every sunlit morning. I hope I was there for you the way you were for me. I can't wait to see you again.

As far as the music, I'm sorry off the bat, but I'm not sorry at all. It's a true hodgepodge of growing up with Avril, My Chemical Romance, Smash Mouth, country music, show tunes, and powerful female ballad singers. If you thought the other things about this party were jarring, just wait until you go from "All Star" to "Defying Gravity" to "She Thinks My Tractor's Sexy." That's gonna weird you out. I hope that the absolute whiplash of emotions will sort of numb you into a sadless haze, and you'll stop crying because you're simply trying to untangle the wires in your brain.

There should be every single type of cheese. A pizza bar. A nacho cheese fountain with dippables. A Coke slushie machine.

Fries of all kinds. Maybe just a short-order deep fryer. Taco bar. Pasta bar. Fresh fruit. Good salmon. Cucumbers with ranch. And ice for every single drink—the crunchy kind that can't chip your teeth.

Do a second round of shots.

Print my face out all huge and play a game of pin the nose on the dead girl. Maybe one more round of shots.

Once you're all lit, bring out the close-up magicians. I want people to be absolutely shocked. I want people threatening to punch a magician in the teeth for ruining the things they thought they knew about life.

Then? Bring out the karaoke. If you've never karaoked before, now is the fucking time. I'm *dead*[2] serious, this is my final request. Sing your heart out, and don't spare a thought for who might be watching. Loose your voice unto the sky. Singing is one of the very best ways to regulate your nervous system when you are, say, grieving and sad. Karaoke will soothe your soul, my friend.

Cheer each other on—put that ridiculous candle app on your phone and hold it in the air. Sing along so loudly that you can barely hear the one on the mic. Come together. Let the lyrics and the music speak for you. Sing something sad. Sing something hopeful. Sing about starting something new.

When everyone has a voice so hoarse they can barely speak, go sit around the fire. Write the things you're feeling and can't let go of on a paper and let them burn. Let the ashes lift into the sky, and I'll meet them there. I'll guide your important, painful things to a place where they can rest. As long as death is in your life, speak to death like a friend who can help. What can time turn over for you? Where can you start anew?

2. I cannot help myself, even now.

If you want to, do. Rest a head or rub a shoulder. Remind each other that life is short, but for today, you are both here. If you need to cry beside the fire, cry again. If you need to laugh beside the fire, laugh again.

Take the time you need as you tell your friends goodnight. Maybe you can let your guard down long enough to share something that you love about another while they are still here. Speak tenderly and softly, and gently touch each other's faces. When you feel low on gratitude, give what you have to someone else. When you feel low on love, give what you have to someone else. It will come back to you, and it will bring its friends.

One last thing before you go—drop your cosmo in the fire. Let the tired, wilted thing find its rest among the flame. It was only ever a flower, bound to end when it began. You might think me cruel for handing you such a fragile beauty, but it was never meant to hurt you. It was meant to help you let it go. So many things can't last forever.

Let all the bittersweet endings stay behind with me. I'll take every single one, and I'll find them a place to be. Don't worry anymore. Remember that you have a lush bed waiting not too far away in a cool room with crisp, white sheets. It's okay that the day is over. It's okay if you need to go to sleep. It's okay that tomorrow will be new, and there will be no big remembering, and I will still be gone. It's okay if the world starts to move on.

You deserve a good night's rest.

Someday when you're driving with the windows down, and you haven't thought of me in a very long time, one of the terrible songs from my funeral will play through your speakers. And maybe for a moment you'll feel your chest knot closed with the sudden grief. Maybe you'll feel the entire weight of what it is to miss someone you cannot reach. And then I hope you'll remember the drunken karaoke, and the kisses in the closets, and the spinning, spinning, spinning. I hope you'll laugh, and offer the pain to the flame in your chest. It will be over before it started. And you'll still be driving with the windows down, while the world keeps spinning, spinning, spinning.

I'll be free and laughing in a field of chocolate cosmos. Take your time with living. I'll see you sooner than you think.

Meet me in the garden . . .

Meet me in the garden
when it's my time.

We'll count the butterflies
and try to remember which color wings meant Grandpa was
    saying hi,
and we'll touch the springtime flowers while you say,

*"I love the texture of these petals. Touch, dearheart. Isn't that
    just wonderful?"*

You will remind me that your father used to own a pharmacy
next to a peony garden when you were just a little girl,

and I'll remember that you told me,
on the day of *your* grandmother's funeral,
you thought you'd die of grief.

"God, I loved that woman."

Then I'll tell you that I can finally understand,
because I thought I would die, too,
when you left so long ago.

But now we're sitting in the garden,
and we're trying to recall what we were so worried about
while we laugh among the butter petals,
like no time has passed at all.

where you gonna go from here?

Can I be totally honest with you?

I think I'm afraid of being successful. I've gotten all right at accepting that good things might leave, but I'm not great yet at accepting that they will come. I'm afraid of things being too good because I don't want to be the reason I lose them. I write this chapter as a final entry weeks after I submitted what I thought was a completed manuscript. Something didn't feel quite finished, and I think I finally know what. I apologize to the many good people who likely rolled their eyes upon me wrestling this beast back from their inboxes for one more pass, but I would be doing you, Dear Reader, a great disservice in leaving it out. I hope that this book is successful, but more so, I hope it is helpful. I wrote it to be the words I needed when I was a bit younger, or in a different spot in my life. Storytelling is a powerful, ancient, and remarkable thing. Those of us who have been given the honor of being a storyteller have a responsibility to use it thoughtfully—to try to add nothing to the world that makes it worse, and to be intentional about trying to make it better.

I've always known *how* I wanted to impact the world, but

I was never set on the method I used to get there. I tried on a lot of hats while I dismissed writing as an option, because the pen never felt mightier than the sword to me, but these days I know the pen is the mightiest thing of all. It still feels absurd to call myself a professional writer, author, storyteller, or anything similar. It still feels like a pipe dream that might vanish in an instant. I'm terrified to say it out loud, like calling myself a storyteller and naming my hopes will scare them off like the neighborhood cat I desperately try to coax to me with *pspsps*, only to watch its indifferent tail disappear into the shrubbery. That devastates me every time. To imagine my career flashing its little cat butthole at me as it saunters away where I cannot follow—making a mockery of my vulnerability and stripped-down desire? I would never recover.

Despite my wild fear of losing everything I never dreamed would be mine, it *does* feel a bit fraudulent of me to allow that very fear to keep me from naming my great hopes. It's a bit shitty of me to simply share what I've *already* accomplished without risking the embarrassment of laying out the goals I may fail to achieve. Like, I don't want to tell you, cuz then you'll know if I'm a failure or not in about three to five business years, ya get me? But I'm going to tell you, because you've stuck with me this long, and it's only fair I trust you if you've trusted me with your time and energy. It's only fair I practice the sort of courage and silly dreaming I preach. So if I'm being as honest as I can be about my secret, fragile hope, what I really want is this: I want to be a storyteller in the largest, most impactful sense. I hope you find me next making television and films that tell stories that change the world. I hope my name is mentioned alongside Phoebe Waller-Bridge and Issa Rae. I hope my work changes the way people think about life, ourselves, and each other. I hope I can give to the world art and conversation that makes it a more kind place to live, and that challenges the ever-living shit out of the bullies and bad guys who get rich on our suffering.

Sometimes I feel like I'm just beginning. Others I feel like everything is bound to end sooner rather than later. Sometimes it feels like I haven't accomplished anything at all. Then I remember that my body of work is not only what's public, but also the many years of pain and change that brought me here. It's not only silly videos on the internet, but also the very real ways that I've connected with so many beautiful, wonderful people. I think I'm not doing very much, then I remember I was in Google's *Year in Search* short film about the possibility of change, and I realize that maybe, just maybe, I'm on the right track and should stop being such an a-hole to myself and minimizing what has happened so far. I am trying to embrace and run toward my big, silly, out-of-this-world-sounding dreams without the fear of failure holding me back, because lots of people can try to stop me, but I'm the only one who can keep me from ever beginning. Where I am now would have sounded like a silly, out-of-this-world dream to me a year ago, and I'm finally done with telling myself no.

What about you, Dear Reader? Is there something wild and new calling your name? Has something broken open for you, leaving you with a new perspective and possibility, and asking you if you'll change? Is there something you want so badly you're afraid to say it out loud?

I hope that you find it in you to name it. Write it on a sticky note and plop it on your mirror. Tell your best friend. Tell your partner. Tell your cat. You'll never sound as silly as me, the girl who *just* told you she daydreams about her Academy Award and Emmy acceptance speeches. And even if you *do* sound as silly as me, make sure you tell your cat about my outrageous dreams too. If you're gonna be judged by a house cat, I can't let you be judged alone.

I'm rooting for you. I'm rooting for me. I'm rooting for us all.

everything the kids
should know

1. Pizza dipped in ranch is better than pizza not dipped in ranch.
2. *Shrek 2* is the best of the franchise and is the most quotable of the *Shreks*.
3. As long as they aren't hurting anyone, people can be into whatever they want to be into.
4. You're going to make a lot of mistakes, and you'll make a lot of apologies too. That's okay.
5. Cheez-Its are the ultimate cheesy cracker, but only the original flavor.
6. You don't need a date to go to the dance.
7. You don't need to go to the dance.
8. It's okay if you don't know who you want to be or what you want to do for a really long time. There's no such thing as the right timeline, only yours.
9. Being kind is a lot more important than being the best.
10. If anyone ever asks if you want to trade your rare holographic Pokémon card for their very average one named Eevee, say no. Eevee is cute, but she's a bad investment.

11. Sometimes it's very important to just shut the fuck up and let someone else talk. You will often have something to learn.
12. Aliens are totally real. Be chill.
13. Wear SPF daily. The sun is a bitch.
14. Your parents will make a lot of mistakes. You're allowed to feel however you need to about them.
15. If there's something you've always wanted to try, make sure you try it. Life is, it turns out, very, very short.
16. Swimming in the ocean can heal many different kinds of wounds.
17. Most things that feel like a really big deal won't feel that big in a few days. Give it a minute before you do anything you can't take back.
18. Capybaras are very cute, but they do not make very good pets.
19. Make sure you buy a quality mattress. You only have one back.
20. Be safe, but not too safe. Life requires a little risk.
21. If it makes you happy, that's good enough.
22. Send flowers to people when they need someone to notice them.
23. Read books and recommend them for someone else to love.
24. Never be afraid to be the first to try something. You can usually try again.
25. As long as it's a mild case, eating cheese is worth the lactose intolerance.
26. The sign of a good lover is how much they love seeing you at home in yourself.
27. Drink your water.
28. Tip street performers for their heart, not their talent.
29. Compassion and curiosity will take you very far.

30. You're allowed to be tough, and also to be gentle.
31. You're allowed to walk away from people and places that make you question if you're a good person.
32. You're allowed to take big leaps.
33. You're allowed to take long rests.
34. You should never, ever get too old to laugh and play.
35. You're allowed to keep on changing.
36. You're allowed to say goodbye.
37. You're allowed to choose love.
38. You're allowed to choose peace.
39. Be your own best friend and confidant.
40. You're allowed to be free.

acknowledgments

In my overwhelming gratitude, I'm not sure what I should say, so I will keep it brief, though I'm paranoid that not naming everyone will make me a certified asshat. I hope you will understand, and I'm sure by now you're sick of hearing me talk in your head.

To the many strangers who have shared with me your love, support, money, time, and stories, thank you for believing in me. You are my heroes.

To the many brilliant people who worked with me on this book, from my agent to my editors, to the entire team at Blackstone, thank you for taking a chance on me. Without your expertise, guidance, and encouragement, this would never have come to pass.

To the many people who have known me, loved me, taught me, and shared with me any small measure of your life, thank you for helping me. I am a mosaic of all the people I've known, and I'm the luckiest person in the world to have known all of you.

And to you, Dear Reader, thank you for giving me the greatest gift of all. Thank you for witnessing my life. I hope that you found something precious to take away from me too.